John:

We hope you'll enjoy looking at the Products of some of our relationships with other clients. We look forward to seeing more fruit of our collaborative efforts with MK.

MK is in my book, an outstanding client.

Elise

M000315247

ARCHITECTURE AS RESPONSE

PRESERVING THE PAST, DESIGNING FOR THE FUTURE

EINHORN YAFFEE PRESCOTT

In memory of Erastus Corning III, Lewis A. Swyer, and Peter D. Kiernan,
who gave us life's greatest gift—an opportunity.

Architecture as Response

Preserving the Past
Designing for the Future

Einhorn Yaffee Prescott

Nora Richter Greer

Rockport Publishers, Inc.

Gloucester, Massachusetts

Copyright © 1998 by Rockport Publishers, Inc.

All rights reserved. No part of this book may be reproduced in any form without written permission of the copyright owners. All images in this book have been reproduced with the knowledge and prior consent of the artists concerned and no responsibility is accepted by producer, publisher, or printer for any infringement of copyright or otherwise, arising from the contents of this publication. Every effort has been made to ensure that credits accurately comply with information supplied.

First published in the United States of
America by
Rockport Publishers, Inc.
33 Commercial Street
Gloucester, Massachusetts 01930-5089
Telephone: (508) 282-9590
Facsimile: (508) 283-2742

Distributed to the book trade and art trade in the
United States by
North Light Books, an imprint of
F & W Publications
1507 Dana Avenue
Cincinnati, Ohio 45207
Telephone: (800) 289-0963

Other distribution by
Rockport Publishers, Inc.
Gloucester, Massachusetts 01930-5089

ISBN 1-56496-410-8

10 9 8 7 6 5 4 3 2 1

Design: Sawyer Design Associates, Inc.

Cover photo: Jeff Goldberg/ESTO
Back cover photos: Walter Smalling, Jr. (top),
Durston Saylor (center and bottom)

Manufactured in China

ACKNOWLEDGMENTS

First, we give heartfelt thanks to our colleagues at Einhorn Yaffee Prescott, both past and present. Your insights, dedication, and hard work have allowed us to produce *Architecture as Response*, and to share our thoughts, dreams, and aspirations with those interested in understanding the potential of the art of architecture to link the past with the future.

A huge debt is owed to Susan Radzyminski, whose intelligence, patience, and belief in the significance of our work resulted in this daunting task coming together.

We thank our talented writer, Nora Greer. Her sensitivity and understanding of architectural issues past and future, combined with energy and an ever-present sense of humor, exceeded our expectations.

Thanks also to Jim McKinney, Mark Warner, and Dennis Drozd for their efforts, and to Diane Sawyer, graphic designer, and all the folks at Rockport Publishers for their confidence and encouragement to tell our story.

Steven L. Einhorn, FAIA
Eric C. Yaffee, AIA
Andrew W. Prescott, AIA

Contents

THE PRINCIPALS OF EINHORN YAFFEE PRESCOTT

W e're not quite sure how it all happened, but it happened. We started our firm in 1973 in Albany, New York. Our goal at the time was to grow to a staff of seven. Today, Einhorn Yaffee Prescott (EYP) totals 400 people with offices in six cities. We began as an architectural firm; today, we are architects, engineers, and interior designers. One of our most important goals is to be recognized as the firm that defines excellence in the seamless integration of A/E design.

EYP's growth is clearly a result of two diametrically opposed actions: our commitment to long-range, strategic planning and our ability and joy in responding quickly and passionately to new opportunities. Underpinning our geographic and project-type diversity is a set of strongly held, firm-wide beliefs and values. First and foremost, we are committed to the operating philosophy that even though we sleep in different cities, we are one firm. In fact, project teams are frequently built across our offices to maximize the unique resources of our professionals. Second, we share a set of values that define our professional environment:

- Extraordinary service to clients
- Commitment to excellence
- Hard work and high individual performance
- Collaborative management style
- Commitment to our people and communities
- Aggressive business development attitude.

The core purpose of EYP's work is to create environments that enrich people's lives. Although project types and opportunities will undoubtedly change in the future because of evolving social, economic, and technological conditions, our core purpose will remain constant. The strong professional alignment of our leadership and our extremely supportive families have

allowed EYP to simultaneously develop a strong and stable business culture and a unique and distinctly focused body of work.

EARLY INFLUENCES

The year 1998 marks EYP's twenty-fifth anniversary. Clearly, Albany, the capital of New York State and the oldest chartered city in the United States (1635), with its rich history and architectural heritage, has profoundly affected the direction and shape of our professional sensibilities. And so has the vision of three individuals—important civic leaders in our community who are deeply interested in preserving our region's architectural landmarks—who became early advocates of our accomplishments in restoration and adaptive use.

EYP milestone projects, such as the restoration of Albany's historic Union Station into Fleet Bank's New York State headquarters and the adaptive use of Quackenbush Square, which saved a collection of the capital's oldest and most historic buildings, were precipitated by the shared belief of Mayor Erastus Corning III, Lewis A. Swyer, and Peter D. Kiernan in our young firm's design capabilities and commitment to architecturally weave our city's history into the future. These early landmark commissions laid the foundation for future historic-preservation projects at Federal Hall, in New York City; at the Old Executive Office Building and the Lincoln and Jefferson Memorials, in Washington, D.C.; at United States embassies and consulates in Rome, Istanbul, and Prague; and at college and university campuses, such as the Massachusetts Institute of Technology, Princeton, Williams, and Georgetown.

Architecture as Response

The remaking or making of architecture cannot be done in a void. For twenty-five years, EYP has engaged in responding to the past while developing planning strategies that embrace the future. Whether we are designing within the walls of an existing architecturally or historically significant structure, adding on or inserting a new building within an existing environment—a neighborhood, city, or college campus—our A/E design solutions strive to simultaneously respect and respond to a comprehensive host of conditions and issues. Our objective as archi-

tectural and engineering designers is to respectfully reconcile what the building or environment was, and what it will become. The new must defer to the old, but at the same time, reveal its own character. Accomplishing a sense of harmony may be achieved through replication or contrast; often the solution requires a combination of the two. Understanding and integrating the spirit and aesthetic qualities of a space into a new environment is a complex and delicate business. For each commission, our design strategies must also respond to the client's/user's needs; thus, each solution becomes a unique melding of an aesthetic and a pragmatic response.

Architecture as Response organizes our work into three sections: building within an existing structure, adding on to an existing structure, and inserting a new building into an existing environment. In each section, our design solutions are discussed in relationship to existing contexts. In support of our belief that a successful solution must respond to both past and future design considerations and user needs, each section is introduced with supporting essays by a leading architecture critic and a prominent building user.

Our Work and Our Process

At EYP, we are committed to a collaborative design process. We believe that a team of highly focused and philosophically linked architects and engineers can produce extraordinarily responsive work. Innovative planning strategies that integrate A/E concepts with a building's past and future are achieved through this design collaboration.

The significance of the work presented in this monograph lies in its collective body of issues and ideas aimed at bringing new life to older buildings and in relating new architecture to existing environments. We hope our ideas and solutions will assist others in exploring design opportunities similar to those we have encountered. Our work is not about style or signature design. In fact, it often involves bringing new functional and technical relevance to signature architectural landmarks. Whether our work should step forward or retreat is simply a matter of reconciling existing contexts, program, and symbolic concerns. We have attempted to include in this monograph a variety of appropriate responses regarding the issue of style.

The work presented on these pages illustrates the efforts of EYP architects, engineers, interior designers, and clients working hand-in-hand. We have been blessed with extraordinary clients and colleagues who have together created a body of work in which we take enormous pride.

THE TIMELY AND TIMELESS

THOMAS FISHER

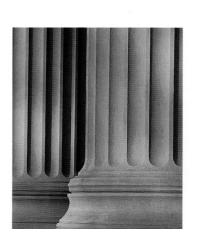

Few architectural and engineering firms have worked on as many important historic structures as Einhorn Yaffee Prescott. EYP's project roster reads like an architectural who's who: the White House, the Lincoln and Jefferson Memorials, the Old Executive Office Building, the Old Post Office Building, Federal Hall on Wall Street, the New York State Capitol. The firm has lived up to the company it keeps. In building after building, its architects and engineers have managed to mix exacting restoration methods with inventive and unobtrusive insertions of new materials and systems.

The significance of this work, however, goes beyond the careful preservation of landmarks. When you look at the scope of EYP's projects—not just preservation and adaptive use but also sensitive additions and delicate insertions of new buildings into an existing fabric—the durability of those structures stands in stark contrast to the lightness and transitory nature of so much of the new construction. Why did Americans, as recently as fifty years ago, construct buildings to last the ages, when what we now build seems intended to last no longer than a few generations?

EYP's work suggests an answer to that question. Many of the buildings they have worked on are Classical not just in style, but in idea. The creation of a "classic"—a standard of something or a model for others—has long been an aspiration in the arts and in architecture. Not only have architects sought to produce classic and enduring works, but their use of the Classical orders and proportions has provided a public and concrete expression of our culture's longing for timelessness. Likewise, the very massiveness of the structures we have built for centuries as our most important buildings has represented our urge to resist the effects of time by creating something that will last forever.

Nothing, of course, lasts forever. Even the most solidly built structures, as EYP's projects demonstrate, demand maintenance and repair. But timelessness is a human idea, not a physical fact, and it is an idea that in this century has begun to wane. Between the industrial revolution and the information revolution, change—rather than endurance—has come to seem the only constant in our lives.

Architecture, an ever-sensitive barometer of our beliefs, has reflected this change. Not only has recent architecture emphasized its transitory nature and changeability, but also it has tried, sometimes too hard, to appear "of its time" or "cutting edge." EYP's architecture does not, and this may be one of the firm's greatest contributions to posterity. Time after time, the firm strives to renew a sense of place, a connection with the past. Whether it is an adaptive use scheme, an addition to an existing building, or a new building set into an existing fabric, EYP responds in a manner befitting the spirit of the place. That doesn't mean the new totally defers to the old.

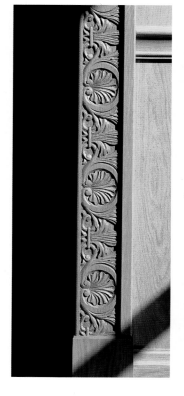

No. The new elements take on a unique expression but one that responds respectfully, harmoniously, and congenially with the old. Additions match the quality and durability of the original structure and admit to the difference between the timeless way in which we once built and the timely way we build today.

Tensions, however, are constantly created by this shift from the timeless to the timely. Nowhere is this more apparent than in our efforts to preserve durable old buildings in a transitory age. Firms such as EYP, for example, must artfully reconcile or negotiate two ideologies, acting as conservators of some parts of these buildings (typically the exteriors and major interior spaces) and as the transformers of others (usually the engineering systems and moveable elements, such as windows). Likewise, architects must try to resolve sometimes irresolvable dilemmas. In deciding how to treat a historic building, for instance, they must weigh the desire to retain the patina of age, which is part of the very appeal of the structure, against the equally strong urge to have it look "like new."

EYP's work reminds us, however, that there is no going back. Once we have seen timelessness as an idea that, itself, exists in time, we can no longer fool ourselves into believing that we can somehow step outside history. At the same time, the firm's work demonstrates that while believing in the value of the past, we also must believe in the value of the future and of leaving something behind us, an idea that the short-term, present-mindedness of so much new construction seems to reject. If we can no longer sustain the belief in the timelessness of Classical buildings, we can still admire their durability and the ambition of their creators to give them as gifts to the future. We might also ask ourselves if we, too, should be giving such gifts, if for no other reason than to avoid being, perhaps justifiably, forgotten. EYP has initiated that dialogue.

RESPECTFUL RESPONSE

Renewing and Reshaping

Preservation of the nation's built heritage is a universally embraced ideal as we strive to perpetuate a sense of place, tradition, and culture. Yet when it comes to the preservation of a single building, economic realities can quickly temper that ideal. How do you successfully preserve the historical integrity of a building and at the same time make adaptations for its continued viability? In other words, how do you make a functionally obsolete building useable in today's high-technology-driven world without destroying its architectural fabric? This dilemma is continually faced by Einhorn Yaffee Prescott in projects that range from the purest restoration to adaptive use. Regardless of the project, EYP's intent is the same: to reconcile what the building was and what it is becoming.

Each building considered for preservation is viewed as a unique structure warranting a unique solution. (The term *preservation* is used here as an all-encompassing word to include pure restoration, renovation, rehabilitation, and adaptive use.) Although the projects themselves vary markedly, EYP's design process does not. First and foremost, a historic building will be most successfully preserved if its future use is identified—and sometimes it will be preserved only if its future use is predetermined. Take Albany's Union Station, for example. Its survival hinged on an agreement that the usable space could be doubled to accommodate the needs of the new owner, Fleet Bank. Otherwise, acquiring this landmark building with its heroic interior spaces would be economically unfeasible. The space requirements propelled EYP to conceive a highly creative plan to meet these space needs and to ensure the historic significance of Union Station.

Of course, any transformation in use will ultimately change a building. The trick is to conceive a plan that successfully alters a historic space without obliterating it. Simply put, one must ask: Can the existing integrity of the building be retained in the conversion? Architectural integrity translates as the qualities of a building or its site that give it meaning and value, such as its style, workmanship, materials, function, massing, and overall continuity and quality. EYP's skill is clearly visible in the New York State Education Building, where mezzanines were inserted into a cavernous space. The result? A human-scaled office environment was created and useable space significantly increased while the dimensions and quality of the original space were preserved.

Through careful analysis, EYP defines those essential elements and formulates ways to preserve and even enhance them. At the same time, strategies to renew the building emerge, depending on where on the spectrum of preservation the project is directed. For instance, in a pure restoration, emphasis will be placed on exact replication of details, such as the work done at Arlington Cemetery's Memorial Amphitheater and the secretary of the navy's office at the Old Executive Office Building. In an adaptive-use project, the goal may be to capture the building's spirit in a way that complements the building's historic fabric and spatial organization. A significant part of EYP's success can be attributed to the fact that it is both an architecture and engineering firm. When each transformation is planned, therefore, the integration of old and new is accomplished through a strategy that simultaneously integrates the architectural and engineering issues into a single design concept.

Two great Albany buildings: one dead and gone to hell, the other decaying from age and disuse.

The dead one was Union Station, built by the New York Central from 1899 to 1900, an era of railroad supremacy, as a monument to financial hauteur; but in the subsequent age of flight and superhighways, the hauteur was humbled. When the failing railroads stopped running trains into Albany, the city's downtown was already collapsing and Broadway outside Union Station, once a crossroads of everybody's traffic and vibrant night life, had turned into a desolate street known for its empty parking lots. The station, empty and boarded up, its tracks scrapped, its roof's copper flashing stolen by thieves, trees growing on that roof, its steel and granite soul eroding from moisture, its walls and 52-foot-high ceiling falling, was a sad and sodden mummy.

The other, the decaying building, was the elegant State Education Building, on Capitol Hill, conceived and built in the years 1908 through 1912 as an architectural superlative (thirty-six marble pillars, each 90 feet tall, 6½ feet in diameter, the longest colonnade in the United States), a worthy next-door neighbor to the architecturally awesome and financially superlative (most expensive building in the United States in 1897) State Capitol.

Capitol Hill was chiefly Washington Avenue, the beginning of the way west out of Albany, the street where nineteenth century capitalists built their mansions; also the street of leftover farmers' hotels and infelicitous houses and stores, all of which went away when the Education Building went up. With its sumptuous sky-lit rotunda, this grand building housed the State Library, whose catacombs were the repository of New York's history. It also housed the State Museum, where every upstate child for generations had been bored by its rock collection, awed by its mastodon, intimidated by its magnified housefly, and transported by its dioramas of American Indian life. Then in the 1970s, Governor Nelson Rockefeller moved library and museum out from behind the colonnade and into the South Mall, his new two-billion-dollar government center across the street; and the Education Building's soul and corpus began to wither.

In 1979, Governor Hugh Carey rescued Union Station with a million-dollar weatherproofing. Five years later, an Albany-born banker, Peter D. Kiernan Jr., decided while shaving that he would save the revered station permanently by making it his bank's headquarters.

In 1987, reacting to pressure by community and political leaders who feared the encroaching obsolescence and decay of Albany's great architectural wonders, state officials decided to save the Education Building from aged irrelevance.

The Albany-based architectural firm of Einhorn Yaffee Prescott was called in to save both buildings—transform the station into a viable bank and transform the empty State Museum into viable workspace for the Department of Education. Subsequent pages of this book detail how this remarkable work was accomplished. Briefly put, the station's usable space was doubled from 50,000 square feet to 100,000 square feet and it was restored to (and beyond) its original grandeur. The restoration has been the subject of a television documentary and has also won fourteen awards, for almost everyone connected to the project.

Into the redesigned exhibit areas of the State Museum, modern curvilinear mezzanines were built for the much-enhanced workspace; the great chandelier in the rotunda, which was falling, was saved from becoming smithereens; the building's skylight, sealed off fifty years earlier to protect museum artifacts from natural light, was restored; and totally new electrical, mechanical, plumbing, and fire-protection systems were installed in the entire building.

The trains, museum, and library are gone forever from these structures, yet the two great buildings are thriving in their new historical roles, their space in daily use, and both the station's erstwhile waiting room and the Education Building's rotunda, in constant demand for public functions. Capitol Hill continues to prevail uninterruptedly as an architectural wonderland, and Union Station (now Fleet Bank headquarters) has brought Broadway back from desolation. A park faces the restored station now, and state and private office buildings have risen as its neighbors.

The greatness of a structure is no guarantee of its endurance (the original Penn Station in Manhattan comes to mind), but enlightened state and cities do, sometimes, successfully practice what might be called spiritual archeology, rooting among mummies and skeletons and infusing new life into what is moribund or even dead. Such buildings were not built as architectural mayflies, for momentary life or fugitive need. They were built in the belief that the city is a permanent thing, worthy of perpetuation. They were restored because the belief was recognized in a latter day and acted upon with great intelligence.

Civilized behavior, you could call this. Not easy to come by.

NEW YORK STATE EDUCATION BUILDING

The renovation of the Education Building is an extraordinary success because the new design enables both efficient and productive administrative work *and* provides an environment that engages us in the glory of the building's past. This exceptional building adaptation permits us to be in two places simultaneously—an office and a museum of memories.

The magnificent renovation of the Fifth Floor is the good fortune and happy consequence of four convergent objectives. The driving force was the creation of the state's

Cultural Education Center in the Nelson Rockefeller Empire State Plaza, which enabled us to build the most comprehensive and impressive state museum in the nation.

Second, as the Education Department's responsibilities and staff expanded in the 1960s and 1970s, office space had to be secured outside the overflowing Education Building. We welcomed a homecoming to advance cohesion among our units and to save rental costs.

Third, we were committed to assuring that Albany's greatest building would continue to stand as a symbol of New York State's exceptional, historic commitment to education. Any adaptation of the building had to be completed with the highest standards of scholarship, historical authenticity, and creativity. It had to reflect a belief in the continuing excellence of educational opportunity for New Yorkers.

Fourth, we were determined that the impact of the former museum as a "downtown" magnet be maintained. Generations of global visitors and New Yorkers—and most importantly, our capital region families—cherished favorite exhibits: the longhouse, the prehistoric forests, and, yes, for some, even the seemingly infinite parade of chickens. When the artifacts moved across the city to the Plaza, we knew we needed to create in their place an inspirational attraction, an "exhibit" of exceptional architectural accomplishment. We wanted visitors to know the Fifth Floor in a new openness that revealed both its original structural marvels and the artistry of its adapted design.

Accomplishing all four purposes presented an exceptional challenge. It required the vision, skills, and painstaking capacity of my gifted colleagues in the Education Department and the Office of General Services. We, in turn, succeeded because of the partnership with Einhorn Yaffee Prescott, who shared our vision and commitment. This was more, much more, than a typical government building project. We were striving for excellence in our home city. EYP understood the role of this incredible building; their members passed by it every day. They understood the sensitivity of completing work of excellence on time, within a limited budget, and right under the nose of government.

Each visit to the building evokes both delight of the beautifully crafted work spaces and memories of the place where we once witnessed with awe the glowing gems, majestic mammoths, and great floating fish. The adaptation is worthy of a great museum and magnificent building, thanks to EYP, and a source of great pride.

The consequences surrounding the birth, decline, near-demise, and rebirth of the New York State Education Building in Albany offer a unique chronicle of how, over time, our regard for heroic buildings changes. Designed by Palmer and Hornbostel and completed in 1912, the New York State Education Building was a grand vision, containing offices, the state library, and a museum. Not only did it reflect advances in technology—it is one of the first steel-framed buildings of its size—it also represented the spirit of its time. Albany was, at the turn of the century, the capital city of a state with unparalleled financial and industrial strength. This monumental, Classical Revival state building signaled the high purpose and hopes of that time, with its vast interior spaces proclaimed on the exterior by a 520-foot colonnade of Corinthian columns, reportedly the world's longest. Now, flash ahead fifty years. Nelson Rockefeller governed a state that, like the rest of the nation, was intent on modernizing. The grandeur sur-

rounding the State Education Building had long worn off. The new esthetic was modernism, and the new Empire State Plaza began draining the life out of the Palmer/Hornbostel building. By the late 1980s, when the building was nearly two-thirds empty, the challenge became one of economics: tear it down or transform it into office space. Yet, the latter seemed an incredible mismatch of building and use.

Einhorn Yaffee Prescott's response centered on enhancing the historic integrity while offering a pragmatic approach to meet the needs of the state. The firm's work began on the fifth floor, the cavernous space that previously housed the state museum. After meticulously surveying the existing interiors, the firm brought together the client and several consultants for a planning session. The team's design concept was to add mezzanines in each of the floor's three main areas. This met the state's requirements to increase the amount of office space by twenty-five percent. At the same time, the mezzanine would float free of the historic elements that defined the space and would allow a seamless integration of mechanical systems.

The mezzanines became bold, undulating, sculptured inserts, shaped to echo the curvilinear geometry and the "museum-like spirit" of the original architecture. The design concept, however, brought an abundance of technical problems. First and foremost, the existing structural system could not support any additional weight. Stiffening the system was too costly, so some clever maneuvers were undertaken. The heavy nonstructural concrete floor decking was removed to "unload" the building. It was then "reloaded" with the mezzanines. Constructed of lightweight steel framing and composite decking, the mezzanines were cantilevered and supported by a series of short unbraced outriggers that extend down to the building's column lines.

The design would ultimately benefit from the rigorous architectural/engineering approach practiced by EYP. The new mechanical systems were carefully woven into out-of-the-way places that did not impede on the historical character of the building. The mezzanine itself contains environmental controls and equipment, and the new floor was raised to allow for accessible wiring. At the same time, the tarred-over skylights were restored. In the east wing, this allowed for an abundance of natural lighting, enough to necessitate banners to eliminate glare on the computers. In the north wing the skylights above the vaulted ceilings were reactivated.

On the third floor, mezzanines were inserted in the two long, narrow spaces and connected by three cross bridges. This preserved views in and out of the great windows, which are twenty feet in diameter and ten-feet high. The central corridor was rebuilt, with ductwork and utility runs inserted in the walls and ceilings.

The classical nature of the State Education Building is proudly announced by its massive Corinthian colonnade and repeated inside in the restored rotunda. The design intent was to reconcile "what the building was and what it was becoming." Permeating the adaptive-use scheme for the fifth and third floors is a respect for the original architectural character.

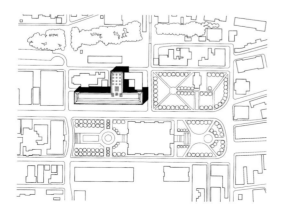

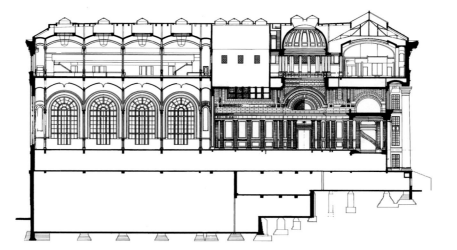

Two conference rooms are located close to the renovated rotunda, which, as seen in the elevation drawing, sits at the heart of the building.

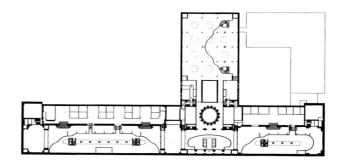

Designed to help control excessive glare on computers, colorful fabric banners catch the direct sunlight entering the east wing of the building's fifth floor through a reinstated skylight. A curvilinear mezzanine provides increased square footage for offices and also provides space for environmental controls and equipment. The result is a visually seamless combination of new and old.

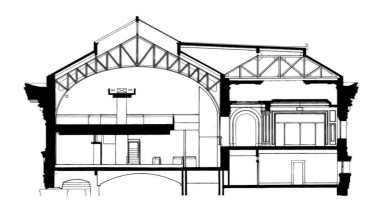

The mezzanine structure was inserted into the formerly cavernous space that had served as the New York State Museum.

Decorative columns and ocular skylights enliven the vaulted space in the fifth floor's north wing and were carefully preserved. As elsewhere, the new element, in this case the undulating mezzanine, was precisely inserted. The new shapes take cues from the old, as seen in the third-floor rotunda and the stair assembly.

On the third floor, a totally rebuilt hallway runs the length of the building and is flanked by mezzanines. Bridges with glass windows run over the hallway and connect the mezzanines. The overall design allows more prominent views in and out of the beautifully restored, monumental tiger-cut oak windows.

Fleet Bank Corporate Headquarters and Data Service Center

ALBANY, NEW YORK

The original, highly decorative surfaces, including two 8-foot (2-meter) plaster cartouches and plaster busts of Elvira that sit at the apex of grand interior archways, were painstakingly renewed by artisans.

Once a grand monument to rail travel, Albany's Union Station would ultimately embody the classic dilemma of heroic landmark buildings. Constructed between 1889 and 1900 and designed by Shepley Rutan & Coolidge (successor firm to H. H. Richardson), Union Station thrived until the 1950s, when new forms of transportation—the automobile and the airplane—drained the life out of rail travel. Although listed on the National Register of Historic Places, this Beaux Arts station was abandoned, vandalized, and suffered nearly to the point of total deterioration. The dilemma? How could this virtually obsolete heroic space be altered for new use without destroying its architectural integrity? Ultimately, Fleet Bank (then Norstar Bancorp) purchased the building on the condition that the useable floor space be doubled from 50,000 square feet (4,500 square meters) to 100,000 square feet (9,000 square meters).

Meeting these programmatic requirements and winning the approval of the State Preservation Office required an innovative space planning strategy on the part of Einhorn Yaffee Prescott. The goal was to skillfully insert a high-technology communications facility and corporate headquarters into the historic structure while maintaining the building's original architectural spirit and fabric. The solution? Reduce the four-story, monumental concourse space to three stories. This meant moving the original cast-iron facades (which once housed ticket booths and offices) inward and upward. Originally 10 feet (3 meters) from the wall, the facades were cut from their moorings, removed, and stored along one side of the lobby. Then they were hoisted up one story onto a new steel structure and set 30 feet (9 meters) from the wall. Thus, the dimensions of the grand lobby changed, but the sense of spaciousness and grandeur was respectfully retained. The first floor became a highly secure computerized nerve center for the bank.

Restoration work on the interior surfaces was extensive and matched the effort made when the building was originally built. Molds were made from the remaining plaster pieces, and several thousand plaster replicas were installed in 3- to 5-foot (1- to 1.5-meter) sections. Of the four original 8-foot-tall (2-meter) plaster cartouches, only one remained. It was cut from its mooring but shattered when it touched the floor. It was then painstakingly reconstructed to act as a mold for the plaster replication. The fluted columns, ornate railings, glass panels, and decorative ornamentation found on the cast-iron facades were restored. Detailed analysis reaching back to original paint schemes revealed dark green and ochre. However, off-white, grays, and Dutch-metal accenting were chosen as more appropriate for an office environment. The mosaic-tiled concourse floor was redesigned based on original drawings and set in dark and light gray and white Vermont marble.

Threading the communications, electrical, mechanical, and security systems into the building without destroying its historical integrity was one of the project's major technical and design challenges. Because the building was constructed without air-conditioning, there was only minimal room for ductwork. Therefore, thin, flat ducts were integrated into floor and wall systems. The electrical-distribution and communications systems were also custom designed and contained in the floors.

So successful was the renovation that now when one enters Fleet Bank, it is inconceivable to think that this elegant, monumental place might have been lost to Albany forever.

The dimensions of the grand lobby were altered in the renovation, as shown in the before-and-after section drawings and photographs. A new floor was inserted and another mezzanine level was created. The history of the grand lobby is illustrated here: the lobby during its train-station era, after ten years of abandonment, and in its newly renovated state.

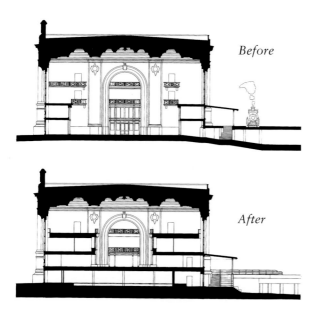

Before

After

The granite facade was in good shape and mainly needed repairs and cleaning. The Broadway Avenue clock was reconstructed around the original numerals that had been found in the attic. Trains stopped at the rear of the exterior, which now accesses a nearby parking garage.

Reception areas were created when new floors were inserted in the three-story wings. New spaces were added to accommodate the bank's needs, including a cafeteria with an outside terrace and an elegantly appointed boardroom and executive office.

Corporate Offices

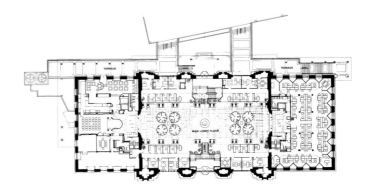

The canopy that once sheltered patrons boarding trains at the rear of the station was replicated to cover a pedestrian walkway to the nearby garage.

The massive Old Executive Office Building now stands proudly amidst extensive site work, including paving, lighting, and fencing improvements. Mullet's design includes nine hundred columns, some Doric and some Ionic, arrayed in porticoes and pavilions. The building is topped with imposing mansard roofs typical of the Second French Empire style.

Few visitors to Washington, D.C., are fortunate enough to have access to the Old Executive Office Building, but all are guaranteed to notice it. The highly articulated and ornamented Second French Empire–style building that sits directly west of the White House demands attention. The massive building has been referred to as a wedding-cake pile of gray granite, a reference to its layer upon layer of Classical details, including some nine hundred Doric and Ionic columns arrayed in porticoes and pavilions. Designed by Alfred B. Mullet and built between 1871 and 1888, the building housed the Departments of State, War, and Navy before it became an annex to the White House in 1948.

The work of Einhorn Yaffee Prescott at the Old Executive Office Building involved the highly visible restoration of the secretary of the navy's office but also much more. Internally, other areas were renovated and an elaborately detailed skylight deep in the heart of the building was reconstructed. Elevators were upgraded to match the 1930s design, asbestos was removed from pipe and ductwork, fire alarm and detection systems were replaced, new sprinkler systems were installed, and air-handler units were relocated. Existing windows were restored and some sash replaced, to provide better energy performance, in keeping with the "Greening of the White House," a program to make the White House and environs as energy efficient as possible. In addition, extensive work was done to spruce up the site, including step repair; stone repaving; rebuilding and repairing retaining walls, fencing, and light poles; and

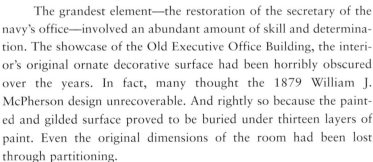

restoration and/or replacement of wood and cast-iron doors.

The grandest element—the restoration of the secretary of the navy's office—involved an abundant amount of skill and determination. The showcase of the Old Executive Office Building, the interior's original ornate decorative surface had been horribly obscured over the years. In fact, many thought the 1879 William J. McPherson design unrecoverable. And rightly so because the painted and gilded surface proved to be buried under thirteen layers of paint. Even the original dimensions of the room had been lost through partitioning.

The availability of historic photographs of the room would prove crucial in its restoration. Workers laboriously removed layer after layer of paint from one portion of the surface to reveal the original colors and patterns on the walls and ceiling and then used this portion as a model for repainting the entire room. Renovating the floor became more complicated when portions of it were damaged by a contractor as the floor was being removed piece by piece. A grand search was undertaken to find mahogany, black cherry, and maple that would match the color and texture of the original marquetry floor.

Removal of the floor was necessary to allow for insertion of advanced security and communications systems appropriate for the room's current and future use—an office and conference room for the vice president of the United States. As with other EYP restoration projects, the introduction of upgraded mechanical and electrical services appears seamless. Existing utility shafts were enlarged to accommodate mechanical systems. Electrical and communication outlets were installed in the original cast-iron baseboard.

Every element of the secretary of the navy's office was painstakingly restored to its original grandeur, which had been lost over the years, including reproduction of the historic chandeliers and, when possible, original pieces of furniture.

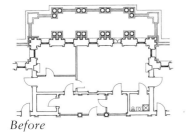
Before

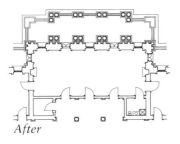
After

Before-and-after floor plans show how the secretary of the navy's office was restored to its original layout. The office is adorned with gilded mirrors and a marquetry floor. Its decorative ceiling was copied from one portion that underwent extensive paint analysis.

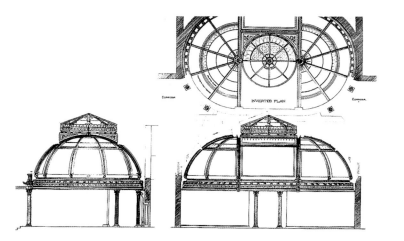

The highly articulated, gilded mirror atop a marble fireplace echoes the ornately painted wall surfaces (opposite). An elaborately detailed skylight deep in the heart of the Old Executive Office Building glistens in its reconstructed state.

WASHINGTON, D.C.

The walls of the library were brought back to their original faux stone appearance—plaster surfaces were textured and painted to resemble stone. Chandeliers were restored and fitted with uplights to place more visual emphasis on the decorative ceiling.

Excessive heat and humidity can wreak havoc on architectural finishes. Such was the case at the U.S. Department of Commerce's Law Library, in Washington, D.C. The library sits at the northeast corner of the Italian Renaissance–style Commerce Building, designed by York and Sawyer and completed in 1932. The climatic conditions in the library did not prove satisfactory, even after an updated HVAC system was installed in 1976. By the time Einhorn Yaffee Prescott was called in for a restoration study in 1989, thermal expansion and contraction of the plaster walls and groin-vaulted ceilings had resulted in severe cracking. Sections of the painted vaults had flaked off, and damage to the west wall of the library was extensive. The once-elegant oak and walnut book stacks had been spoiled.

Careful examination revealed that in spite of the damaged and flaking areas, the stencil-painted ceiling decorations were generally in good shape. The restoration team painstakingly cleaned the vaults by hand with kneaded erasers to preserve the original paint and finish. Areas that had been damaged were repainted; the undamaged portions served as color and texture models. Period chandeliers were restored and new uplighting was delicately inserted.

Special consideration was taken in upgrading the climate control systems for the room. Based on library design standards, a twenty-four-hour HVAC system was designed with special humidification and dehumidification controls. It was inserted on the adjacent courtyard roof and, therefore, did not interfere with the historic fabric of the library's interior. New bronze air-register grilles were matched to the room's single remaining original grille.

FEDERAL HALL NATIONAL MEMORIAL

George Washington proudly guards the spot where he was inaugurated first U.S. president. A Greek Revival structure with a Roman-style interior, Federal Hall features a central rotunda, where formal receptions are often held.

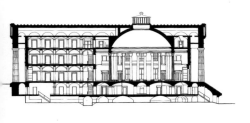

Not surprisingly, all landmark buildings eventually face a common quandary: how to update antiquated internal engineering systems without sacrificing the historic integrity of the structure. Such was the case when the National Park Service approached Einhorn Yaffee Prescott to analyze conditions at Federal Hall, make recommendations for an improvement program, and design an engineering system upgrade. Located in the heart of the city's Wall Street section, Federal Hall is a Classic-style marble Greek temple built in 1842 as the U.S. Customs House on the site where George Washington was inaugurated as the nation's first president.

Modeled after the Parthenon, Federal Hall contains the offices of the National Park Service as well as classrooms and a museum. It is the third structure on the site. The first was constructed in 1703 as New York City's second city hall. It became the first U.S. capital in 1789, when George Washington was inaugurated. That structure was demolished in 1812 and replaced by a small brick building that served as the U.S. Customs House. The third building, designed by Ithiel Town and Alexander Jackson Davis, once housed the U.S. Customs House and a sub-treasury. The Greek Revival structure features Doric columns and a porticoed entrance, in front of which stands a large bronze statue of George Washington. Its interior is derived from Roman building styles and features a central domed rotunda that rises 54 feet (16.5 meters) and is encircled by sixteen Corinthian columns. It was designated a national memorial in 1955.

EYP's plan called for the upgrading of internal systems—heating, ventilating, and air-conditioning. To assure energy efficiency and a favorable savings-to-investment ratio, life-cycle analyses were undertaken. Because of the landmark status of Federal Hall, all architectural and engineering design strategies had to be accomplished without affecting the building's historic integrity and in accordance with federal preservation standards.

MEMORIAL AMPHITHEATER, ARLINGTON NATIONAL CEMETERY

ARLINGTON, VIRGINIA

A pronounced gateway frames a first view into the classically inspired amphitheater. Fronted by the Tomb of the Unknown Solider, the reception building (right) marks the amphitheater's eastern entrance.

The Memorial Amphitheater was a structure tearing itself apart, having suffered from a long history of water damage and well-meaning but ineffective remedial work. The challenge was to develop a new waterproofing and roofing system to accommodate movement due to the building's varying thermal range, and allow water drainage from behind the stones. In all, some 400 drawings and forty-three treatments were developed to restore the stone elements.

The Memorial Amphitheater was designed by Carrere and Hastings and built between 1915 and 1920 on a prominent site in Arlington National Cemetery, in Arlington, Virginia. Clad in white Imperial Danby marble from Vermont, the elliptical-shaped, Classically inspired amphitheater accommodates 5,000 people and is fronted by a formal reception hall. The amphitheater's roofed colonnade is made of marble pilasters on the outside circumference and, on the inside circumference, 30-inch (75-centimeter) load-bearing marble columns built over a basement crypt. The amphitheater seats are white Vermont marble. The colonnade, stage, and floors are white Vermont and pink Tennessee marble on a mortar setting bed.

The restoration work began with a review of the original construction and subsequent repair drawings. Then, physical investigation involved visual, water spray, and nuclear surveys of the leaks, along with sonic tests, core-sample tests, and microscopic examination of the marble. These revealed that thermal expansion and inadequate control joints had caused horizontal displacement and shearing of the stones. Cracks in columns raised questions about the capacity of the marble to support the loads. The reinforcing steel structure was rusting and the natural cements were dissolving. Calcite deposits had formed in the micro-cracks of the stones and in their concrete backing and were causing the stones to slowly explode. In addition, the deposits caused orange and yellow stains on the marble, which under examination by a medical microbiologist, were identified as a bacteria. A chemical treatment was developed to abate the bacteria. Gradually, the unwanted coloring will dissipate. There was significant loss to some of the decorative carving because of weathering. The marble was also stained green from copper and had rust stains from ferrous metals and ferrous minerals in the stone.

Four renovation alternatives were recommended. The Army Corps of Engineers implemented the most extensive renovation plan, which entailed patching, cleaning, and replacement of some stone. Steps and paving were reworked to allow for waterproofing and flashing. The arcade roof and drainage system were replaced.

Careful cleaning, special treatments, and replacement of marble brought the serene luster back to the amphitheater's surfaces.

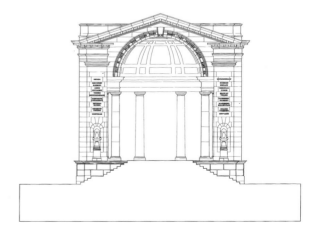

WASHINGTON, D.C.

At dusk, the Lincoln and Jefferson Memorials take on a soft glow. Careful study was undertaken at both monuments to determine the extent of deterioration and to plan for future restoration efforts.

The National Park Service is a highly conscientious conservator of our national heritage. So when the lower portion of a volute fell from an Ionic capital at the Jefferson Memorial, questions arose about the long-term physical viability of the monument. The Park Service deemed that a comprehensive survey of existing conditions was needed and turned to Einhorn Yaffee Prescott to determine the cause and effect of various types of deterioration. Subsequently, EYP's investigations were broadened to include the Lincoln Memorial. Both studies will be used to direct any future renovation work undertaken by the Park Service.

Designed by John Russell Pope and dedicated on April 13, 1943, the Jefferson Memorial was inspired by Jefferson's own Classical architectural preference. The superstructure is Vermont marble, with Georgia Tate marble walls surrounding the Rudolph Evan statue of Jefferson. An in-depth analysis of the monument revealed emerging patterns of deterioration, discoloration, and wear, as well as differential movement of building elements. EYP determined that external influences, such as induced vibration from helicopters overhead and the nearby Metro trains, and routine maintenance activities also have played a role in the wear and degradation of stone features. Implementation of EYP's recommendations is being phased in, with new roofing already in place and stair and stone-wall repair currently underway.

Designed by Henry Bacon and dedicated on May 30, 1922, the Lincoln Memorial, with its unpedimented Greek Doric form, is perhaps the best-known national monument in the country. The Lincoln Memorial faced similar degradation and wear problems as the Jefferson Memorial, and its study concentrated on documenting the more than 8,000 individual pieces of cut limestone and marble load-bearing stones, as well as decorative, or cladding, marble. This database will be used to record future maintenance efforts and to monitor the effects of long-term weathering on the building. On EYP's recommendations, the skylight systems have been reconditioned and the flat roof replaced. Much effort was made to study the cause and extent of damage to the Jules Guerin murals that cover the walls flanking Daniel Chester French's statute of Abraham Lincoln. Questions remain about whether the existing, but no longer functioning, heating system originally installed behind the murals should be reactivated in an effort to stop the paint deteri-

oration. In addition, an extensive study was launched to find possible solutions to the midge problem at the memorial. The Lincoln Memorial is infested with midges—small bugs that swarm at dusk and are attracted to the monument's lights. This study ultimately involved an entomologist who actually attached sensors to a midge and tested the bug's reactions to different types of light and lighting schedules.

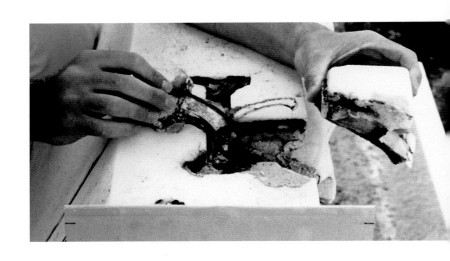

The condition of each of the more than 8,000 pieces of cut limestone and marble blocks comprising the Lincoln Memorial was documented. Inside, the cause and extent of damage to the Jules Guerin mural flanking the statue of Lincoln was investigated.

Lincoln Memorial

Jefferson Memorial

At the Jefferson Memorial, analysis revealed emerging patterns of deterioration, discoloration, and wear, along with differential movement of building elements.

ALBANY, NEW YORK

*A dynamic, five-story central
atrium becomes the bridge and
circulation zone for the two
adjacent buildings and fully
announces the design's "industrial aesthetic."*

When relocating its offices in the late 1980s, Einhorn Yaffee Prescott did what came naturally. The firm chose to restore and adapt three adjacent historic buildings in downtown Albany. This response was a conscious effort to support the revitalization of New York's state capital city, whose downtown experienced its heyday in the late nineteenth century but saw much of its livelihood migrate to the suburbs in the latter part of this century. Underused, the historic city's collection of landmark buildings remains largely intact. The Argus grouping, which housed the Argus Press until 1912, and the magnificent Renaissance Dutch building across Broadway Avenue, also saved from destruction to become the administrative headquarters of the State University of New York, now anchor the historic district's southeast corner.

Over the years, the Argus Press had occupied three adjacent structures built at different times in different styles: an 1856 Italian-style building at the corner, an 1867 unadorned flat-front brick in the middle, and an 1888 Richardsonian Romanesque facade at the end. Combined, the buildings offered a generous total of 30,000 square feet (2,700 square meters). But because each steps slightly uphill, the three were never internally aligned. Later, a fourth building that runs the length of the three would add an additional 5,000 square feet (450 square meters). The buildings, however, were in generally good condition. Adequate roof maintenance mitigated the structural deterioration that often appears in older buildings if moisture penetrates over several freeze-thaw cycles.

EYP determined that the internal horizontal alignment problems could be solved through the building's renovation. The center building was totally gutted and redesigned as a central atrium. Walk inside and the volume dramatically explodes upward five stories. A new, intricate bridge and stair system works to seamlessly connect the complex's uneven floor heights. Vertical circulation is provided by a glass-enclosed elevator with a stairway wrapped around it.

Once gutted, the structure of the center building revealed itself—heavy timber beams and posts set atop a cast-iron frame on the ground floor. This interplay of bold lines seemed to evoke the building's industrial origins, so the structure was purposely left exposed throughout the interiors. Added to that structural grid are steel columns around the elevator shaft and steel railings in the atrium; in the offices are exposed steel duct work, pipes, and lighting systems.

All the while, from the exterior, the buildings retain their historic image. Working closely with the New York State Historic Preservation Office, EYP made only one major modification. To serve as a new entrance to the three buildings, an arcade was carefully tucked into the ground floor of the middle building, a facade that had previously been altered. Although still appearing to have three separate facades, the building's new entrance symbolically ties the complex together. The service alley was closed off to traffic and paved in brick, a paving that is carried into the lobby. Otherwise, the exteriors were carefully cleaned, and weather-beaten limestone lintels and corner corbels were replaced.

The white-painted brick walls of the centrally located atrium serve as a neutral background to the grid of exposed wood beams and iron girders, an image that changes drastically with time of day and different view points.

The loft's design vocabulary is carried into the executive office, which shares the fifth floor with the library. One of two original spiral staircases still provides additional floor-to-floor connection.

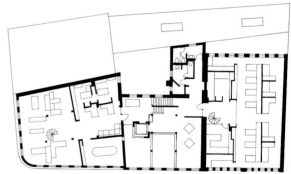

GENERAL ELECTRIC COMPANY WORLD CUSTOMER RECEPTION CENTER

General Electric's Building 37 holds a unique position in the company's history, as well as the nation's. This is the site where the first industrial research facility in the United States generated technological ideas that led to revolutionary developments in electric lighting, radio, and TV broadcasting. Now the building, with the massive GE sign at its top, has become an international customer service and corporate training center. The renovation by Einhorn Yaffee Prescott played on this duality—it sought to reinforce the historical role of GE through a careful renovation of the exterior and to highlight the company's current technological leadership in the state-of-the-art interiors.

GE's historic Building 37 is announced by a massive black glass billboard bearing the original company logo. A concrete canopy provides a new ceremonial entrance, which leads into a modern lobby.

Built on top of the Erie Canal in 1925, Building 37 was designed as an industrial, utilitarian building. As the GE research and development operation grew, Building 37 was gradually vacated for more modern labs at a new R&D campus. Building 37 became virtually obsolete and sat unoccupied for several years.

In the renovation, the only radical change to the exterior was the addition of an entrance canopy skylight, a structure that provided a much-needed ceremonial entryway into the building. Made of concrete to sympathetically blend with the concrete-and-masonry structure, its design was kept simple to reflect the industrial theme of the building.

The interiors, however, were brought up to 1990s standards and beyond. The 16-foot (4.9-meter) ceiling heights allowed for great planning flexibility, and insertion of new mechanical, electrical, and communication systems proved to be relatively uncomplicated. Between all offices, there is now instantaneous paperless communications. The second and third floors are the most utilitarian and house the Customer Engineering Operations staff. The fifth floor, housing the Human Resources and Corporate Council Departments, and the sixth floor, housing the GE Power Division senior management staff, were designed in association with Carol Grohe Associates. These two floors are more finely appointed and carefully integrate natural lighting and wall systems with a rich palette of natural materials and bold colors.

The first floor is the building's showcase—the GE World Customer Service Center. Containing a 200-seat auditorium, conference rooms, and training rooms, the layout is highly flexible to meet changing technological and user needs. The main lobby announces the high-tech energy of the division with brushed aluminum ceiling and polished granite floors.

*The interior design of the fifth
and sixth floors revolves around
bringing natural light deep into
the interiors. Design elements
include transparent wall screens
and bold colors on the fifth
floor and more subdued tones
on the sixth.*

A formal gate announces the Freshman Quad, of which Sage and Williams Halls comprise three sides. The residential halls were restored and preserved to secure their original design intent.

SAGE AND WILLIAMS HALLS, WILLIAMS COLLEGE

WILLIAMSTOWN, MASSACHUSETTS

At Williams College, tradition and quality go hand in hand—two characteristics that are reflected in the buildings on campus. Take Sage and Williams Halls. Forming three sides of a gated quad, these turn-of-the-century, Gothic Neo-Georgian residence halls house a large portion of the freshmen on campus. The desire for updated, quality housing led to the decision to renovate. At the same time, Williams College desired that the spirit and sense of tradition of the quad be maintained, which ultimately meant redoing the interiors without sacrificing the halls' original vertical entry stair and suite organization.

For Einhorn Yaffee Prescott, the goal was to successfully walk the fine line between accommodating the future and respecting the past. A complete exterior restoration brought the three-story buildings back to their original appearance—red brick, limestone trim, slate roofs, and ornamental copper work. Most important, the entry system stayed the same—a series of single-door entries that lead to vertical stairwells. The interiors were gutted, equipped with updated electrical, mechanical, and ventilation systems, and reorganized into suite arrangements, which were, for the first time, linked horizontally to comply with code requirements. Every two suites share bathroom facilities, a radical departure from the original design that had all the bathrooms in the basement. The interiors were finished with white plaster walls and wood trim in a new expression of the old.

The most radical departure from the original structure came about because of the need to add beds lost in reworking the floor plan. To accomplish this, the grade of the basement level of Williams Hall was lowered to allow natural light in and views out of new quality living spaces. The altered elevation was seamlessly integrated with the original.

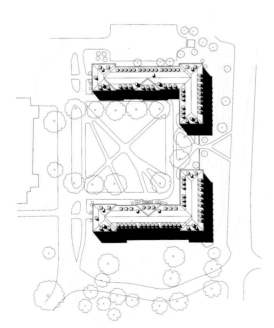

*The floor plans were reconfigured
to provide modern suites with
a "traditional" design spirit.
Single- and double-occupancy
rooms surround common
living spaces.*

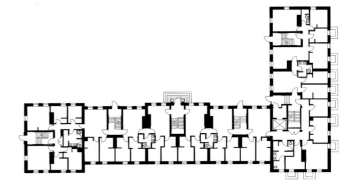

Kirby Hall, Lafayette College

While the Classical exterior of Kirby Hall will be carefully restored, the interiors of the 1930s building will be brought up to modern educational standards.

When it was dedicated in 1930, Kirby Hall was one of the finest academic buildings constructed on an American college campus. Designed by Warren and Whetmore, Kirby Hall is a superb example of the Classical Revival style of architecture popular in the early twentieth century. It takes many of its proportions and details from Classical Greek architecture. Not surprisingly, over the years, it became an architectural and historic landmark, anchoring the southwestern portion of this campus north of Philadelphia. In addition to housing academic functions, the building also became the museum for the Kirby Art collection. Constructed of the finest materials—Indiana limestone, travertine, bronze, and oak—and well maintained, the building has worn well. In fact, no major repairs have ever been made. But even the best has limitations. Lafayette College turned to Einhorn Yaffee Prescott for a comprehensive feasibility and design study to bring the hall's facilities up to modern standards.

Of major concern is the need to provide a sophisticated, modern environment for teaching and research. For Kirby Hall, all internal systems need extensive upgrading and new systems need to be added for data, communications, and electrical support for technological improvements, as well as for air-conditioning and environmental control. In addition, the facility needs to be brought into compliance with the Americans with Disabilities Act to be accessible to handicapped students.

EYP designed improvements to be thoughtfully integrated into the existing building with minimal visible impact to its historic character. Therefore, exterior and interior details of architectural and artistic significance will be carefully preserved and protected during renovation and as new systems are integrated into the building. The renovation of certain components, such as the refurbishment of the limestone exterior, may be deferred if there is useful service life remaining or if deferring work would have little or no impact on operations within the building. The hope is, after all, that if Mr. Kirby returned to the building bearing his name he would find it much improved, but not altered.

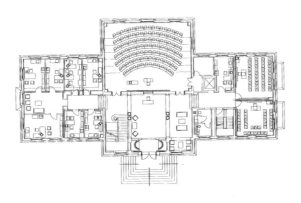

A building-envelope restoration plan will be the end product of EYP's analysis of ten Classical Revival buildings designed by William Welles Bosworth that comprise the heart of the MIT campus. Of particular concern is window and dome restoration.

MASSACHUSETTS INSTITUTE OF TECHNOLOGY, MAIN GROUP RESTORATION STUDY

CAMBRIDGE, MASSACHUSETTS

At the heart of the Massachusetts Institute of Technology (MIT) campus are ten Classical Revival buildings designed by William Welles Bosworth and constructed between 1915 and 1938. Forming a magnificent symmetrical grouping set around a series of courtyards that open to the Charles River, the buildings feature a unique, counter-balanced, double-hung, steel-sash window system designed by Bosworth to provide ample daylight and ventilation and to preserve the planar appearance of the facade. The restoration of these windows, along with the building envelopes and roofs, will be no small task. Just consider the 2,500 windows and skylights or the miles of limestone and masonry that cover the 938,000 square feet (84,420 square meters) of buildings. Such a project deserves a prudent approach, as Einhorn Yaffee Prescott proposed to MIT. Through careful analysis and study, EYP will examine options available to MIT in refurbishing the buildings—that is, to restore, repair, or replace components. Integral to those options will be factors of ease of use, appearance, historic design, maintainability, and initial and long-term cost.

Currently underway, the investigation's first step involves a preliminary survey of thirty windows to establish basic window types, details, design and construction, and potential for restoration. Many sashes and frames show significant corrosion and are no longer operable. EYP's initial investigation also includes a thermo-scan of the entire envelope to identify areas with high levels of moisture for further investigation, along with a preliminary survey of the roofs and domes and a hazardous-materials sampling.

With all the data in hand, an interdisciplinary team convened for a day-long session to establish methodology and goals and choose a smaller team to perform a "mock down." As the third step, the mock down involved the disassembly of sample windows to see how they are put together and anchored and to test techniques for hazardous-materials abatement, paint removal, metal surface preparation, and recoating. At the same time, an extended survey of four hundred to five hundred windows continued, with information entered into a computer database for use in preparing cost estimates and in evaluating repair and replacement options. Evaluation of the

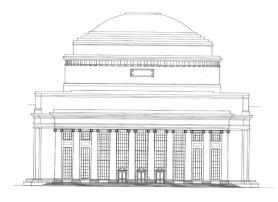

total masonry envelope identified the range and degree of any facade program, such as cracking, rust, stains, and efflorescence. Finally, options for the different window types were developed with cost estimates and evaluation of life-cycle costing, which will be reviewed during a second interdisciplinary meeting. The final proposal identifies capital investment, life expectancy, and future maintenance costs of alternative restoration strategies.

Renovation of Blair Hall will assure its place as a centerpiece on the campus of Princeton University. The exterior features a semi-coursed ashlar or local schist embellished with cut limestone details.

BLAIR RESIDENCE HALL, PRINCETON UNIVERSITY

PRINCETON, NEW JERSEY

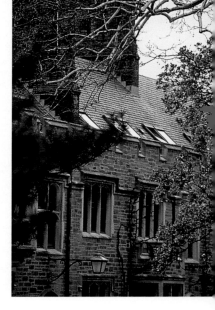

To understand how architecture can establish a sense of place, one need only look at Princeton University's Blair Hall. The residence hall, built in 1896, immediately brought a collegiate atmosphere to the campus. And because it borrowed its aesthetic language from English Collegiate Gothic, it added a permanence far beyond its own years. Now, a century later, the esteemed university is looking to Einhorn Yaffee Prescott to extend the life of the building through a renovation of its interior and a careful restoration of the exterior.

The original architects, Cope and Stewardson, modeled Blair Hall on Magdalen College, in Cambridge, England, relying heavily on the use of cut stone and limestone for the exterior. The entire building is faced with a semi-coursed ashlar of local schist, embellished and protected with bush-hammered cut limestone copings, quoins, opening surrounds, belt courses, and finials. The limestone is most extensively used in arches and ceilings of the main portals and for the decorative carved panels, bosses, figures, and grotesques that adorn the two towers. Exterior restoration will involve masonry repair, window repair, and replacement and repair of the slate roofs.

Interior renovation of the 75,000-square-foot (6,750-square-meter) building may be more extensive. For example, the current communal toilet facilities that are located in the basement will be replaced with new toilets located on each floor. This may necessitate the removal of some interior bearing and nonbearing walls and a partial reconfiguration of the current room layout. Alterations to entranceways will be required to bring the building up to current codes, as will replacement of all mechanical systems, plumbing, and fire-protection systems, and an upgrade of electrical systems. All this will be accomplished with as little disruption to the historic fabric as possible.

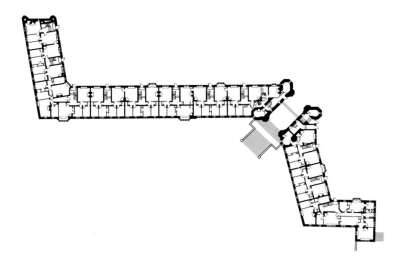

College Hall, Gallaudet University

At the apex of the building, the restored lyceum evokes the Victorian spirit of the original interiors and provides an elegant setting for small meetings of the administrative staff.

For the last century, College Hall has stood as a centerpiece of Gallaudet University, one of the country's premier colleges for the deaf, located in Washington, D.C. Built in two stages between 1863 and 1875, the Victorian Gothic structure once housed dormitory rooms, a museum, and a recital hall. But the original splendor of the interiors had been slowly eradicated as new uses brought temporary partitions, awkwardly placed ceilings and sprinkler systems, and so forth. For Einhorn Yaffee Prescott, the process of renewing those interiors was one of discovery. Exterior work involved the removal of all intrusive, nonhistoric elements, as well as repairs and replacement of masonry, windows, and details.

The designers searched through archival drawings and photographs in their attempt to restore the interiors to their original state. They discovered incredibly pristine elements hidden under temporary plaster or plasterboard walls—the main stair's decorative cast-iron railing, Gothic-style columns in the original museum, and even covered-over stained-glass windows. In fact, the former museum space was entirely re-created out of a series of "cubbyhole" offices and a corridor whose walls encased the gothic arches and columns that now span the room. This room now serves as the reception office of the university's president. Replacement stained-glass windows, decorative tiles, and lighting were copied from whole or partial remnants, as were the original color schemes. The recital hall, or lyceum, was the greatest surprise of all. An acoustical ceiling had been inserted into its spectacular two-storied, vaulted-ceiling space, and its wooden ceiling had been desecrated.

To bring the building back to life as the administrative hub of the campus meant integrating new mechanical, electrical, and communication systems in an unobtrusive manner. New systems were installed in soffits and baseboard raceways, eliminating the surface-mounted systems that had been added over the years. The building was air conditioned for the first time in its history with a two-pipe, fan-coil system that was selected to replace the steam radiators because of its relatively small impact on the historic architectural fabric.

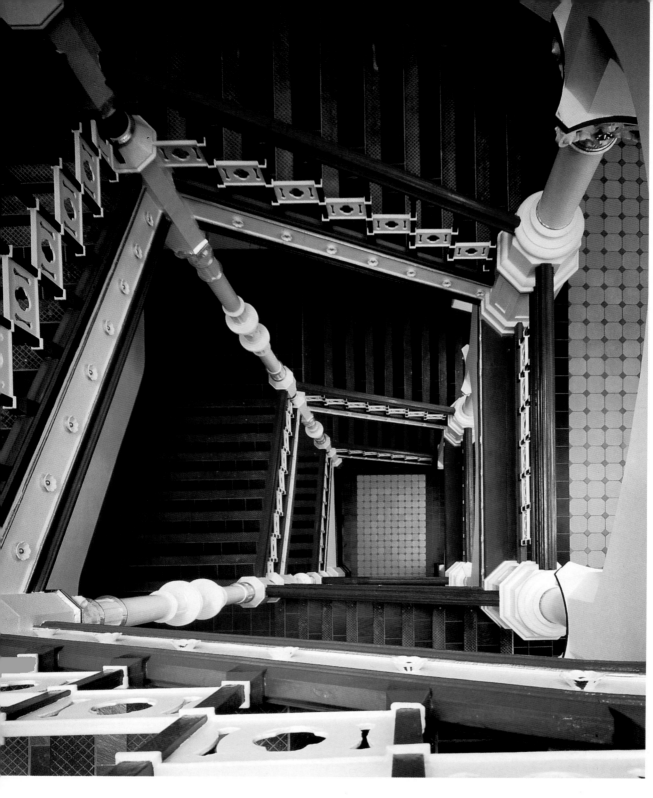

The restoration released hidden elements of the cast-iron staircase, as well as ornate columns, bold arches, and stained-glass windows, as in the president's office (above) and a hallway.

Several Renaissance-style buildings comprise the Rome embassy (opposite, top and bottom right). The U.S. ambassador in Buenos Aires is housed in the Bosch Palace (below), and the U.S. embassy's main residence in Prague is a 1920s mansion (opposite, lower left).

In foreign countries, the embassies of the United States are often housed in palatial structures of historic value to the sponsoring country. For the U.S. Department of State's Office of Foreign Buildings Operations, this presents the ticklish dilemma of how to insert modern engineering technology and security systems into these elegant buildings without altering their historic integrity. To ensure seamless design solutions that address these complex architectural and engineering challenges, Einhorn Yaffee Prescott has been engaged to work on several historically significant buildings, including the Rome embassy and the U.S. ambassador residences in Buenos Aires and Prague.

For the Rome embassy, EYP is evaluating the architectural and engineering systems throughout the existing compound and its perimeters to enhance security and public access control. Located on a 4.52-acre (1.8-hectare) site, the American embassy in Rome consists of several Renaissance-style buildings, the oldest of which dates back to the 1600s. Great care has been taken by EYP to devise approaches for inserting modern systems without compromising the building's historic fabric and without incurring unnecessary costs. Each area—from the most ornate to the most utilitarian—will receive a unique integration of architectural and engineering design strategies.

In Buenos Aires, the American ambassador resides in the Bosch Palace, a French Classical building constructed in 1911. A major landmark, the 33,000-square-foot (3,000-square-meter) palace is considered an important symbol of the relationship between Argentina and the United States. A comprehensive investigation of existing conditions determined the following interior and exterior renovation needs: restoration of facades, windows, doors, ornamental metal shutters and railings, and damaged relief sculpture; restoration of finishes and decorative elements; renovation

of the kitchen; conversion of staff quarters to offices; and an upgrade of the HVAC, plumbing, lighting, fire-protection, and electrical systems. For exterior restoration, special laboratory analysis compared the new stucco with the old stucco, to match the existing stucco in texture and color.

In the Czech Republic, the American ambassador resides in a mansion built in the late 1920s by Otto Petschek, the patriarch of one of Czechoslovakia's wealthiest families. The 50,000-square-foot (4,500-square-meter) building has been found to be in generally sound condition and features a winter garden, state dining room, numerous salons and gathering spaces, as well as administrative and residential spaces. Improvements will include an upgrade of mechanical and electrical systems, renovations to structural systems, and restoration and preservation of decorative elements and finishes.

WARNER MUSIC INTERNATIONAL, U.S. CORPORATE OFFICES

NEW YORK, NEW YORK

An understated elegance is apparent throughout the headquarters of Warner Music, located in historic Rockefeller Center.

Inserting high-profile corporate offices into a world-renowned office complex is no easy feat but one sensitively executed by Einhorn Yaffee Prescott. The landmark is New York City's Rockefeller Center, called the finest spatial grouping of skyscrapers in this country and maybe the world, comprising nine buildings with dominant, continuous vertical piers on three city blocks with surrounding plazas. Construction began in midtown Manhattan in 1929, on a design by Reinhard and Hofmeister with Harvey Wiley Corbott and Raymond Hood, architects. For its new U.S. corporate offices, Warner Music chose not to repeat the building's original exuberance but opted for a restrained and understated elegance, a timeless aesthetic that doesn't compete with the building's renowned spaces, such as the exuberant Art Deco lobby decor and Radio City Music Hall interiors.

This timeless elegance is created through the use of neutral and natural finishes. The subtle palette of beige and off-white is used throughout the 34,000-square-foot (3,060-square meter) space on the seventh and eighth floors of 75 Rockefeller Center. Here, EYP inserted private, glass-enclosed offices along the building's perimeter and elsewhere created open offices, conference rooms, listening rooms, production studios, and workrooms. Attention to daylight was an important consideration in the design, as a shift in light provides subtle changes in depth and texture. Furniture is lacquered in the palette's soft colors; the office cubicles are light-colored wood; and the conference room is a richer oak. Built-in, glass shelving systems contain selections from the company's collection of compact disks, which become spots of bright colors and bring focus to Warner Music's accomplishments.

HARMONIOUS RESPONSE

ADDING NEW TO OLD

Designing an addition to an existing building can be risky business. How do you respond successfully to the aesthetics of the original building, which surely have some intrinsic value? Do you replicate the existing architecture, echo its massing and materials through a contemporary idiom, or contradict the original with opposing forms and palette? Or what if the original structure functions well but needs new clothes? How much do you borrow from the language of neighboring buildings? For Einhorn Yaffee Prescott, regardless of the problem and the approach applied, the goal is to create a sense of harmony between the new and the old, to renew the spirit of a building or its place in a larger community.

EYP's response is influenced by several factors. First are the user's needs. Why is the client seeking an addition? To add more space, connect several buildings, or redesign the entrances? The parameters of these new spaces will play a defining role. A small addition might echo the building's original character; a large one might take cues from the original but stand on its own as a contemporary building; or vise versa. The decision to contradict or replicate must be carefully explored on a project-by-project basis.

Obviously, the character of the original building and its location within the community or campus are other reference points. If it is a historic structure or even a quality "background" building, the goal may be to offer an addition that seamlessly merges with the original. Take the Albany School of Humanities, for example. There, a friendly, early 1900s, brick-and-limestone neighborhood building was doubled in size without much disruption to its environment. The addition sympathetically recalls the original language, but special elements make its newness known. In the case of the Veteran's Administration Medical Center, in Northport, New York, EYP developed a design approach in which a major building addition reestablishes the campus's Georgian Revival theme that had been fractured through insensitive planning decisions. Urban-renewal projects are also categorized as additions, for surely these projects give added value to their locations. For both Canal Square and Quackenbush Square, EYP looked to the urban context for clues to the new amenities.

Added value is of particular importance to EYP. Not only does the firm produce an addition that harmoniously responds to the original building, it also strives to provide extra value in its design solution. Take Gifford Hall, where EYP sculpted an outdoor amphitheater next to the building—an open-air theater that draws users from the entire Middlebury College campus and symbolically links the building to the geology of the site. At Colgate University, EYP turned a nonfunctional dining hall into a space filled with ambiance, the use of which goes well beyond simply dining.

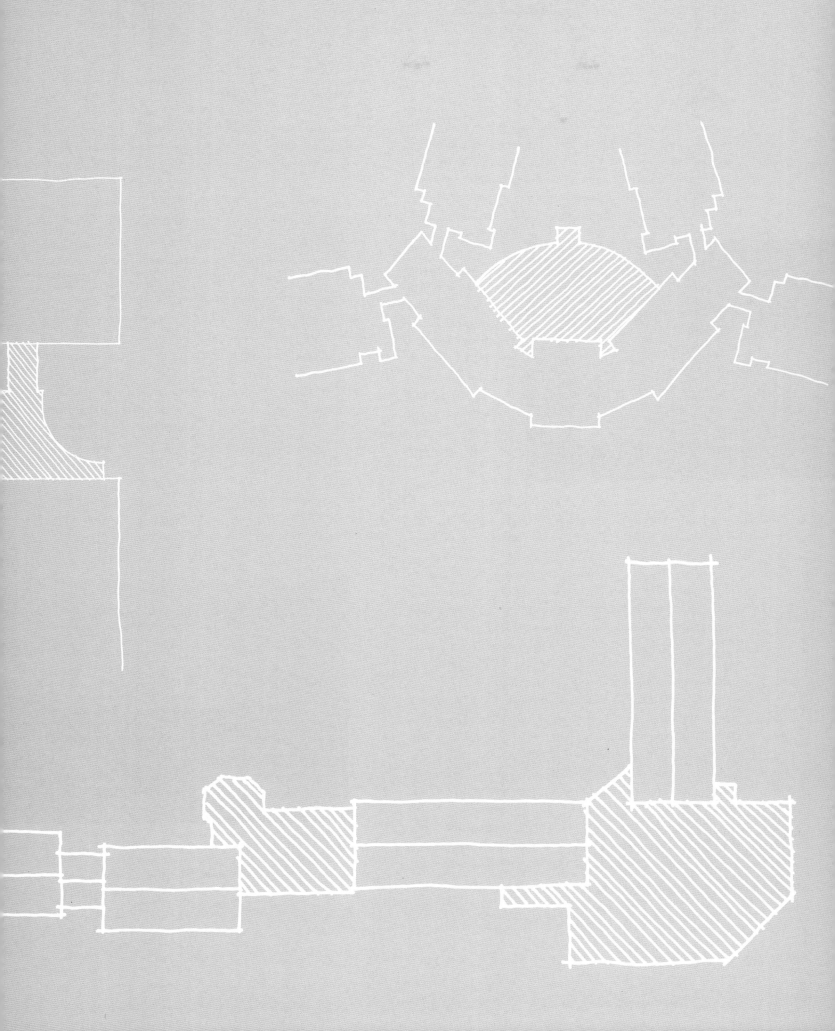

CRITIC'S VIEW: CHARLES LINN

ROSS COMMONS RESIDENCE HALLS, MIDDLEBURY COLLEGE

As a rule, architects are so aware of whether a building works in its particular context that they can make a judgment about its appropriateness and recite the reasons for success or failure within a matter of seconds. To the general public, context is something more visceral: They look at a building and instinctively know that it fits or it doesn't, although they might not know why.

Often, their judgments are just as valid as the architect's. What makes the difference between whether or not a building fits into its context? In a word—patterns. Do the materials complement one another? Do they fit into a larger ensemble that reflects a tradition that might date back 100 or 150 years? Are the proportions of the building's massing and fenestration right? Does the layout of the building make sense in relation to the other buildings around it?

The Modern movement in architecture sought to remove buildings from any sort of context whatsoever. And although it gave architects complete freedom to design whatever they wished, it sometimes produced buildings that were unsatisfying to their users. They were different, unfamiliar, and at times ignored the users' functional and emotional needs. They simply didn't fit.

The Milliken, Hadley, Kelly, and Lang Residence Halls comprising Ross Commons at Middlebury College, in Middlebury, Vermont, were built in the late 1960s and 1970s and were devoid of the college's strong architectural context. Gone were Middlebury's traditional materials (stone and clapboard), architectural patterns and rhythms, and finely crafted details, such as cupolas, dormers, and porticos, which are reflected in the adjacent academic buildings and in the nearby village of Middlebury. The residence halls were constructed of wood curtainwall and exposed concrete.

When Einhorn Yaffee Prescott was approached with the challenge of renewing the residence halls and lounge and capturing the context that had always been missing there, they responded by studying stone-and-clapboard-clad buildings in the vicinity, as well as by looking at how the buildings, when tied together by in-fill, would create a traditional court in front of the buildings. This would subsequently provide a much-needed exterior edge to help define the south campus. Local granite, lead-coated copper and slate roofing, and white-painted wood siding re-create the material patterns that are expected in this context. Window and entry systems, inspired by traditional patterns and shapes, also weave these buildings into the Middlebury campus, village, and countryside contexts, helping students and alumni feel that they belong.

EYP's philosophy of creating buildings that are sensitive to pattern and context has a somewhat altruistic by-product that users of those buildings may never overtly sense but is, nonetheless, extremely important to the principals of the firm and their associates: The design intent of these buildings should clearly reflect the architectural traditions and environmental conditions of a region, and this clarity should be carried on by the designers who will add on to the campuses or buildings designed by the firm in the future.

ROSS COMMONS RESIDENCE HALLS, MIDDLEBURY COLLEGE

Middlebury College, a small, liberal-arts college in Vermont's Champlain Valley, is a residential, campus-centered college that relies on the diversity of talents and interests among our student body, faculty, and staff to enrich the learning experience and extend it beyond the classroom. Maintaining the quality and appeal of the buildings on the 200-year-old campus is, therefore, extremely important. Recognizing the need to renovate many of the older residence halls, the college conducted a self-analysis in 1983 that would serve as the foundation on which the long-range dormitory renovation program was developed. Assumptions and objectives were developed through the evaluation of the residence halls relative to their cosmetics, conveniences, energy conservation, and life safety, as well as to major maintenance goals. The needs expressed by the Faculty Committee on Long-Range Planning and the Residential Life Council concerning the integration of academic and social interaction within the residence halls were also addressed.

Einhorn Yaffee Prescott was invited to orchestrate the renovation and restoration of Gifford Hall in the fall of 1988 and successfully developed a fully renovated, 160 bed, 52,000-square-foot residence hall within a three-month time frame. The results are remarkable. Faced with the prospect of upgrading the Milliken, Hadley, Kelly, Lang complex—three freestanding buildings comprising 88,000-square-feet and 385 beds—the college once again turned to EYP for its expertise.

Middlebury College approached EYP with four goals: Accomplish an architectural aesthetic and construction quality that will be worthy of renovation after 100 years; make a unique and special contribution to the quality of the Middlebury campus; create a complex that will stand at the top of the room-draw list of members of all classes—in other words, be the most desirable residences on campus; and provide for the inclusion of students, faculty, and staff participation in the planning process.

EYP's solution accomplishes that—and much more.

Early on, we realized the wisdom of our choice. We couldn't have been more pleased and excited by the interactive process that EYP undertook in developing the project. The firm set up an office on campus and began a series of formal and informal meetings, encouraging input from all those who participate in university activities—students, faculty, and staff. This process provided EYP with a clear vision of additional goals for the gut-rehabilitation—including significantly upgrading the quality of living; creating the most desirable residences on campus with home-like finishes, comfortable heating, and natural ventilation and lighting; and organizing the site to provide improved outdoor areas for students. Perhaps most important, we felt totally involved in making decisions about a major building project.

Not enough can be said about the success of EYP's design in regaining the collegiate spirit of Middlebury. Bringing the exterior appearance of the residence halls in line with Middlebury's traditional image, as well as making friendly gestures toward the rural vernacular, has cemented the western edge of the campus and created a presence that was lacking before. Ross Commons has worked magnificently to encourage that interaction among students, faculty, and staff that we cherish.

In the renovation, four residence
halls were connected and their
concrete frames were clad in
Corinthian granite from a local
quarry. In the process, vernacular images were incorporated
into the design.

MIDDLEBURY, VERMONT

Founded in the early nineteenth century and set in the Green Mountains of Vermont, Middlebury College's growth into a prestigious liberal-arts school was matched by the construction of collegiate buildings clad in locally quarried limestone. Yet this architectural tradition was discarded in the early 1960s with the construction of dormitories clad in concrete and wood. The

four buildings comprising Ross Commons—known as the Milliken, Hadley, Kelly, and Lang Residence Halls—were designed in that era's ruling aesthetic of modern design by a prestigious architect. By the late 1980s, however, these buildings didn't respond well to students' needs. Internally, the dormitory organization was not appropriate for students' expectations of privacy, nor was the austere finish of the surfaces attractive to the more comfort-driven students. Even more curious, the four buildings were thought an eyesore, a rude intrusion on the campus. The prevailing sentiment was to tear the complex down.

Instead, EYP took advantage of what the buildings had to offer—a sound structural core of reinforced concrete walls attached to a concrete frame and set on bedrock. The solution was to totally gut the buildings, reorganize the floor plans, connect the buildings, add more common space, and reclad the exteriors in materials that reinforced the architectural heritage of the campus. The choice of cladding material was significant. Because the local limestone used elsewhere on campus was no longer available, Corinthian granite was chosen for its lively range of colors. A pinkish-colored Stony Creek granite is used as a contrast at the lintels and sills. This use of locally available materials reinforced the college's ideal of sustainable design.

Internally, the floors had been organized vertically around stairwells and bathrooms. Rooms were small; the insulation was inadequate; and the acoustics were poor. No adequate social spaces

existed. Clearly, what was needed was a more horizontal alignment of rooms, a variety of room types and common spaces, and a linkage between the buildings. All was accomplished, and in the end, the bed count was raised from 385 to 405.

The two new links added a sense of presence to the complex. Set between Kelly and Lang Halls on one side and Hadley on the other, the first link features a five-story tower structure clad in granite. The tower overlooks a new outdoor common, created where a service road once existed. The second link—set at the apex of the 90-degree angle between Hadley and Milliken—repeats the tower image; but this time, it's clad in white clapboard and engaged by a one-and-a-half-story, shed-roofed building. This second link houses the Ross Lounge, which contains a room large enough to accommodate the complex's entire residential community. The Ross tower offers an anchor and a new gateway at the west end of the Middlebury campus.

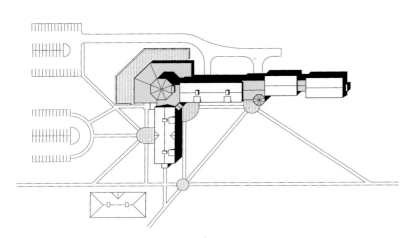

Extensive landscaping created a
sweeping lawn in front of Ross
Commons, removing the paved
street that previously ran close
to the residence halls.

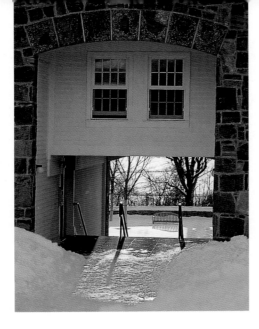

Passageways tunneled through the residence hall buildings facilitate outdoor access through the buildings.

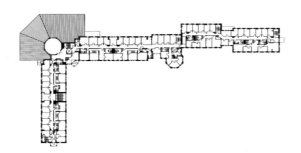

A powerful image in itself, the Ross Commons tower anchors the west side of the campus (opposite). An abundance of natural light enters the interiors of the complex, as seen in a residential lounge and room.

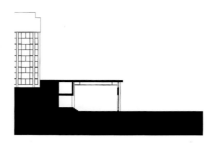

Before

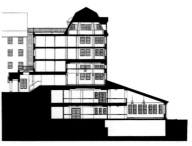

After

GIFFORD HALL AND ANNEX, MIDDLEBURY COLLEGE

MIDDLEBURY, VERMONT

The limestone-clad Gifford Hall proudly sits on a rocky ledge and looks out over the Middlebury campus. Design elements of Gifford Hall and its annex are echoed in the new marble-clad link, which replaced the smaller link (below).

Gifford Hall presented a similar, although less complex, renovation problem at Middlebury College than did the Ross Commons residence halls. Built in 1940, the limestone exterior was in excellent condition and complemented the traditional campus image, but the interiors at Gifford were antiquated. The building's internal systems had outlasted their useful life; the interior spaces were dark and dreary; and the interior floor plan did not accommodate the lifestyle of today's students. In addition, the five-story Colonial Revival structure lacked adequate communal space and was physically cut off from the three-story annex that housed seminar and classroom facilities.

Much of the improvements suggested by EYP cannot be seen from the outside. For example, the internal floor arrangement was reorganized to include a variety of living arrangements from single rooms to suites, and the communal bathrooms were replaced with individual bathrooms. The residential capacity of the five-story dormitory was increased from 156 to 162 by reclaiming storage space in the attic and basement. New mechanical and electrical systems were carefully woven into the building's framework.

Multilevel lounges were added at the ends and center of the corridors to increase the amount of community space and allow more natural light to enter the building. A colorfully decorated coffeehouse was inserted into the basement in space excavated out of the bedrock, and this social gathering space was carried outside into an open-air amphitheater. The coffeehouse/amphitheater thus becomes Gifford Hall's distinctive community amenity, responding to Middlebury College's tradition that each building provide a unique contribution to the character and quality of life on campus. A sky-lit, marble-clad, two-story link was also inserted between Gifford Hall and the annex building.

Symbolizing the building's connection to its bedrock foundation, a stone ledge is left exposed in the amphitheater and carried inside to become a decorative element in the coffeehouse.

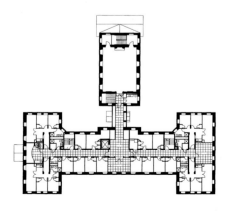

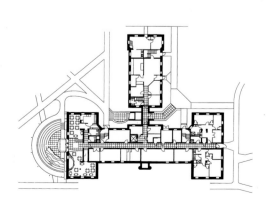

Natural daylight floods the interior of the new link between Gifford Hall and its annex. The newly created coffeehouse and amphitheater significantly enhance the campus amenities and are favorite gathering places.

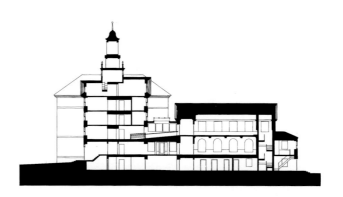

ALBANY SCHOOL OF HUMANITIES

When the City School District of Albany established a new magnet school for the humanities, a wise decision was made: Invest in the development of a physical facility so keyed to the program's mission for grades kindergarten through six that it could only enhance the educational experience and gain the support of the entire community. Einhorn Yaffee Prescott responded with an award-winning solution that heightened the school's mission to "integrate the multicultural and global aspects of art, language, literature, and music within the mandated curriculum" while sensitively respecting the needs of the surrounding residential neighborhood.

Chosen to house the Albany School of Humanities (ASH) was a 1925 elementary school, a 60,000-square-foot (5,400-square-meter), brick-and-precast-concrete building set in a residential neighborhood. Fortunately, city-owned property nestled at the rear of the school accommodated an addition of the same size, and provided ball fields and playground space for school use. Sensitively conceived in the same materials and similar massing, the addition visually makes a modern statement yet blends seamlessly in with the old to create a coherent whole.

A new arcade (opposite) adorns the front of the building. Doubling the space of the existing elementary school, the addition employs similar materials and massing to blend seamlessly with the old. A cylindrical entry visually ties the old with the new.

Set at the back of the building, the U-shaped addition extends the original building's circulation patterns. The center of the U becomes a voluminous indoor courtyard covered with a vaulted, metal roof. In essence, the back of the old school becomes an elaborate set design for the new stage of the multifunction room. Adding to the drama, windows in the old school overlook the courtyard as do bay windows on the second floor of the addition. Designed to accommodate up to seven hundred people, the courtyard space is used by other schools and members of the community. A cylindrical entry drum marks the entrance to the multifunction space and works to visually connect the old school to the new addition.

A thoughtful adaptation to the original school was the transformation of the former auditorium/gymnasium into a state-of-the-art media center. Designed to evoke a sense of classicism and "living literature," the renovation brought back brilliance to the intricately painted design icons on the walls and the vaulted barrel ceiling, newly lit with cove lighting.

In a friendly gesture to the neighborhood, the original main entrance was enlivened with a covered arcade configured like open arms. The main student entry was expanded and now a sweeping ramp carves out an area for a child-size wooden bench. Special amenities include the location of all prekindergarten and kindergarten rooms in reclaimed basement storage space with on-grade, direct access to a protected play area. Music rooms received special acoustical considerations. Project rooms provide flexible expansion space for special temporary projects. New TV, telephone, and data systems are integrated throughout the building.

Seen from the rear, the addition takes on its own identity. There, each of three function spaces presents a unique expression to the residential neighborhood. The cafeteria is a curved form, the gymnasium is a large box punched with glass block, and the music area is a skewed rectangle. Inside, these forms become a series of destinations clustered around the central courtyard.

The dynamic multifunction space was created as the heart of the school. The back of the old school acts as a stage. Colorful banners add even more spirit to this naturally-lit space.

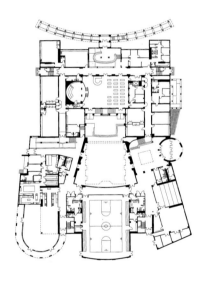

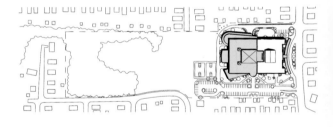

Facing a residential neighborhood, the back of the addition appears as a series of different yet interconnected buildings taking the form of a curved volume, a large box, and a skewed rectangle. The cafeteria, a multistory space, is encircled by a covered arcade.

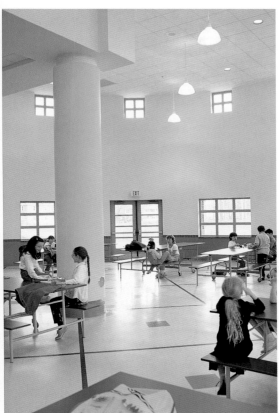

Much different in feel, yet just as grand as the multifunction room, is the media center. Restoration and adaptation of the existing auditorium/gymnasium (below) reawakened the Classical details of the original architecture.

Students wait in the new lobby (opposite) for transportation home. The kindergarten students have their own playground located just outside the colorful classrooms. Other classrooms overlook the media center.

THE EDGE CAFÉ, COLGATE UNIVERSITY

The multicolored floor becomes a bright, decorative focal point during dining hours and doubles as a dance floor when the hall is transformed into a disco. Once under-used, Bryan Hall is now one of the most popular gathering places on campus.

The transformation of Colgate University's underused Bryan Dining Hall into the popular Edge Café illustrates how bold conceptual design can maximize and even add value to low-budget projects. Bryan Hall was constructed in 1966 as a common eating space for 160 students from four residential halls and consisted of two utilitarian dining rooms separated by a shared kitchen.

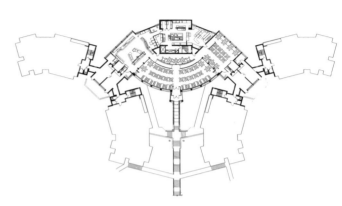

The university turned to Einhorn Yaffee Prescott to gut the dining hall and redesign it as a friendlier space. EYP went a step further and clipped on a fan-shaped pavilion that elevated the dining hall to one of the most popular multifunction spaces on campus.

In retrospect, the insightful solution seems readily apparent. The curved addition increased the space by 3,000 square feet (270 square meters), bringing seating capacity up to 250. At the same time, it drastically improved the ambiance of the dining experience.

The design solution, geometry, and integrated, flexible lighting system allow the space to function not only as a dining room, but also as a coffeehouse, disco, and meeting/lecture facility.

The new pavilion-like dining room, with its exposed trussed ceilings and curving walls, has an open, airy feeling, which is articulated during the day by an abundance of incoming natural light through large windows and a ceiling monitor. An 18-inch (46-cm) difference in floor level between the new and existing construction permits an elevated stage, or conversely, a sunken dining area. The stage, in turn, is further defined by a space frame that supports theatrical and fiber-optic lighting and a raised roof that features clerestory windows. A brightly colored and patterned dance floor is the focal point. The variety of lighting choices—ambient lighting by incandescent downlights, gem lights, uplighting with fluorescents, and neon lighting—brings the opportunity for great changes in mood.

Fronted by a portico entrance and edged with the large windows that previously donned the old dining rooms, the café has become a beacon, a welcoming space. It is announced by a formal stair, which bridges the steeply sloping topography.

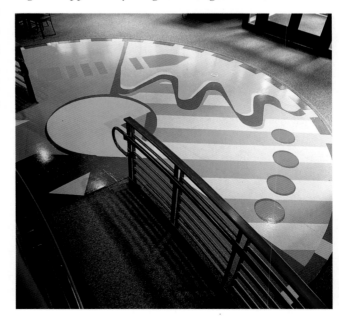

A space frame supports theatrical and fiber-optic lighting, and a raised roof features a clerestory window, all of which provide a variety of moods to the multifunction space. The newly formed "stage" is backed by an existing brick wall.

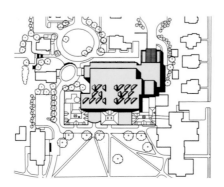

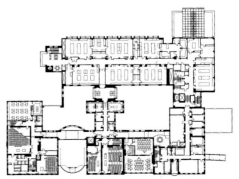

Since the most recent science facility was built at Williams College some thirty years ago, the entire science program has nearly doubled in size. The college, therefore, faced the need to expand and upgrade its facilities to maintain the strong presence the scientific disciplines had earned. An ingenious solution does just that and will consolidate the various sciences and promote interaction among the departments.

The design calls for an 80,000-square-foot (7,200-square-meter) addition to be placed south of the three Thompson Laboratory buildings, each of which are nearly one hundred years old, and the thirty-year-old Bronfman Science Center. (Einhorn Yaffee Prescott is completing this project in association with the architectural firm Zimmer Gunsul Frasca Partnership of Portland, Oregon.) At the center of the old and new elements will be the science library, envisioned as the "spiritual hearth" of the science complex. To be open twenty–four hours a day and to contain all department collections, the library is designed to act as a catalyst for increased interdisciplinary activity. Surrounding the library (and, in many cases, overlooking the library) will be the teaching labs. The concept here is to facilitate the interplay between the literature research and empirical investigation that characterizes the scientific method.

To connect the Thompson buildings, the floors of which vary in level, glass-enclosed ramped corridors will skirt the southern facades of the Thompson labs and will overlook the library. Bridges will connect the new complex with Bronfman. To minimize the apparent mass of the addition, which sits next to smaller houses, its southern facade will comprise oversized and recessed glass. To respect the facade of the Thompson labs facing the science quad, the entrance to the addition facing the quad will be a clear glass curtain wall.

The new science center will unify all the scientific disciplines into a unique structure in which new elements will connect older science buildings. From the science quad, the addition will appear as a curtain glass wall and allow views of the Thompson Laboratory buildings.

New entrances will take the
form of glassy extensions,
transparent elements that
will not diminish the original
Edward Larrabee Barnes-
designed residence halls.
New meeting rooms will
be tucked into the rear of
several buildings.

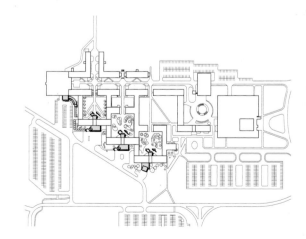

RESIDENCE HALL COMPLEX, ROCHESTER INSTITUTE OF TECHNOLOGY

ROCHESTER, NEW YORK

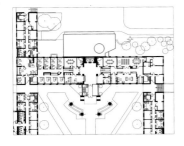

In the process of adding new to old, the stakes are raised a notch when the existing building will someday be considered a historic landmark. Such is the case with a complex of thirteen residence halls designed by Edward Larrabee Barnes and constructed between 1966 and 1972 at Rochester Institute of Technology (RIT). Not yet old enough to be listed on the National Register of Historic Places but in need of renovation and additional space, Barnes' design brought immediate respect from Einhorn Yaffee Prescott. In turn, EYP's response is highly deferential to the original architecture.

The most difficult design challenge is creating new entrances and providing a large space for seminars and social functions. The entrance towers will be the most visible addition and will be glassy extensions. This will allow the Barnes design to remain prominent and also will allow light to enter underground tunnels that connect the residence halls to a dining facility. The meeting rooms will be tucked into the rear of several buildings and defer to the massing and materials of the Barnes buildings.

A series of tunnels currently connect the basement levels of all residence halls, which provides a convenient, but undeveloped, enclosed "street." To enhance the attractiveness of this unique feature, which could be quite enticing in Rochester's severe climate, several changes are planned. New entrances to the tower buildings will introduce natural light to the tunnel to clearly mark the major access points. Seminar room additions will open to the parking lots and greatly improve access to elevators. Finally, the tunnel will be extended to reach a major destination point, the Grace Watson Dining Hall.

CANTON, NEW YORK

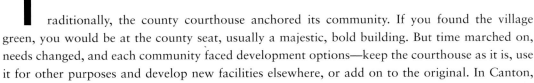

Traditionally, the county courthouse anchored its community. If you found the village green, you would be at the county seat, usually a majestic, bold building. But time marched on, needs changed, and each community faced development options—keep the courthouse as it is, use it for other purposes and develop new facilities elsewhere, or add on to the original. In Canton, New York, St. Lawrence County underwent a growth spurt. In 1924, a clerk's annex was constructed in a manner sympathetic to the original 1803 Richardsonian-style courthouse. A boxy, one-story addition was built in 1958, a building that failed to enhance the original courthouse's image. In fact, the addition was so inappropriate that in the early 1990s, the county commissioned EYP to provide new facilities for the court that would surround that unattractive box.

The courthouse addition is a complementary, contemporary rendition of the 1893 Richardsonian courthouse. A torch light, surrounded by a central stairway, is a dramatic presence in the new lobby.

The new addition takes its cues from the original courthouse—its sense of scale, fenestration, and materials. For instance, the gray manufactured stone simulates the appearance of the original Gouveneur marble, a material that is no longer available. Brown-colored cast stone at the foundation, belt coursing, and trim matches the Potsdam Brownstone of the old. The new is not an exact replication of the old but rather a welcoming reinterpretation, with its arcaded ground level and prominent entrance. It becomes a pleasant appendix, and in fact, the addition was pushed back to allow the original building to regain its prominence.

Inside, the addition takes on a contemporary look, with hints of the old. The focal point is a two-and-a-half-story, centrally located lobby, the tile floor of which borrows geometric patterns and colors from the old. The lobby's volume, as well as that of the second-floor criminal court, echoes the 1893 courtroom. The new family and civil courts are less grandiose in scale but not lacking in fine appointments. Located at the rear of the addition, a drive-through sally port and a key-operated elevator provide for secure transportation of prisoners and separate circulation for judges and jury.

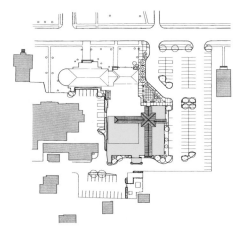

An eclectic grouping of twenty interconnected wood-frame buildings, the hotel was fully reconstructed to its original appearance.

West Virginia has its Greenbrier; Indiana has its French Lick; and Vermont has its Equinox Hotel—grand hotels that reflect a unique regional architectural and cultural heritage. Each has been painstakingly preserved, and now the complexes thrive as resorts and conference facilities.

Development of the Equinox Hotel reaches back to 1801, when its doors first opened. The original hotel would grow over the next one hundred years to become an eclectic grouping of twenty interconnected wood-frame buildings that formed a small village. The resort became known widely for its spectacular natural setting and gracious hospitality. That was until the 1970s, when outmoded accommodations, deteriorating facilities, and a decline in the travel industry forced its closing. It would lay dormant for ten years, exposed to the natural elements and vandalism.

Because the restoration and rehabilitation of the hotel received federal funding from a federal Urban Development Act grant, as well as preservation tax credits, the project involved a collaborative effort among the owner, The Galesi Group; the architect, Einhorn Yaffee Prescott; and the Vermont State Historic Preservation Office. The goal was to preserve the historic fabric of the buildings while providing new amenities. This meant that the exteriors were meticulously restored and the interior was rehabilitated to include 154 guest rooms and suites, a tavern, formal dining room, shops, and conference facilities.

The collaborative effort began with extensive cataloguing of the historic buildings. Most of the foundations had collapsed, requiring the buildings to be supported during renovation. The post-and-beam, balloon, and conventional framing systems were sound in some instances and had failed in others, requiring individual solutions on a building-by-building basis. The design of a four-story, wood-framed guest wing set at the rear of one of the original buildings deliberately complements the existing hotel buildings. The most difficult task proved to be inserting new

HVAC and fire-protection systems in the low-ceilinged structures. Also, one-quarter of the southern wing was destroyed or damaged by fire when that wing was close to completion. In the end, with the help of nearly 150 skilled local craftsmen and laborers, the Equinox Hotel was restored to all its glory. Visiting there now is a timeless experience.

The original lobby and formal stairway were restored to bring back the regional flavor and playful opulence of the original interior. A complementary, four-story guest wing was added at the rear of the existing hotel.

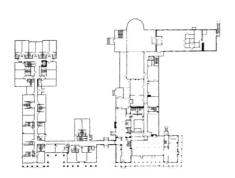

CANAL SQUARE

The development of Canal Square was like performing open-heart surgery on a dying patient. The town of Cohoes, like so many small, Northeastern mill towns, had witnessed the decline and deterioration of its once-vibrant core. The festive Canal Square pumped new life—and new hope—into the very heart of the four-block central business district.

With no potential private-sector interest on the horizon, the city decided to invest in itself by rebuilding its central city infrastructure and by adding public amenities. The investment to attract private-sector development paid off. Canal Square has transformed central Cohoes from a bleak, deserted urban landscape to a bright public space, appropriate for festivity and repose. Its main features are a grouping of concrete, open-air kiosks set near an open-air

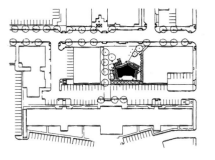

amphitheater; a fountain; and a wading pool. All these elements work to draw in pedestrians, particularly when the weather in the upper Hudson Valley cooperates. The details of Canal Square were meticulously planned, from the brick paving to the new street lighting, planting of trees and flowering plants, and inclusion of bus-stop shelters, benches, drinking fountains, and information booths.

In preparation for the urban surgery, Einhorn Yaffee Prescott performed an in-depth analysis of the existing physical elements of the four-block central business district. The analysis included a historic and architectural review of all existing structures, a study of pedestrian and vehicular circulation patterns, and the identification of future development parcels. Recommendations for the general upgrading of all public spaces highlighted improvements to sidewalks, lighting, landscaping, graphics, street furniture, and parking facilities. Structural additions, such as the kiosks and bus shelters, take design cues from the adjacent civic buildings.

The festive amenities of Canal Square have brought renewed attention to the heart of downtown Cohoes.

A large clock marks the entrance
to Quackenbush Square, which
leads back to an outdoor café sheltered by a wooden trellis.

Quackenbush Square, like Canal Square, is an excellent example of a city investing in its past to secure its future. An important part of Albany's original footprint exists in the city's oldest structure—Quackenbush House—a 1730s struc-

ture that was nearly lost to demolition. It was the city's Mayor Erastus Corning III who championed the idea that Quackenbush House, and the complex of buildings surrounding it, could once again become part of the city's active urban life. Thus, with the support of the New York State Department of Transportation, the Federal Highway Administration, and the U.S. Department of Housing and Urban Development, and a successful urban-design concept, Quackenbush Square is now home to restaurants, a museum, a planetarium, and a visitor's center, all woven

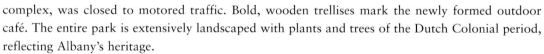

together by an urban cultural park.

Einhorn Yaffee Prescott's approach was to reconstruct the deteriorating complex in its original image as much as possible. Quackenbush House, the smallest of the three structures, was renovated into a quaint restaurant. The other buildings, including the Albany Water Department's 1872 administrative building and 1894 operations building and shop facility, were in various states of disrepair, including fire damage. In each building, structural walls were left in their original positions and new interior spaces designed around them. Repairs were made with materials the same as or complementary to the originals. To create the new public gathering place, Quackenbush Street, which bisects the complex, was closed to motored traffic. Bold, wooden trellises mark the newly formed outdoor café. The entire park is extensively landscaped with plants and trees of the Dutch Colonial period, reflecting Albany's heritage.

The master plan for the B&O Railroad Museum skillfully blends new buildings with old—the 1884 roundhouse and a new interpretative center will serve as focal points.

The B&O Railroad Museum, one of the oldest and most prestigious railroad museums in the United States, stands at the crossroads. If conservation of its buildings and rolling stock are not undertaken, the museum will lose the valuable heritage it is trying to protect. If the museum chooses to implement the master plan created by Einhorn Yaffee Prescott (with museum consultants Sears and Russell), the complex has the potential to become one of the greatest railroad museums in the world and a major tourist attraction for visitors to Baltimore.

The museum was created in 1953 by the Baltimore and Ohio Railroad, with a collection—rolling stock, archival materials, and small artifacts—dating back to the 1830s. In 1987, the main-

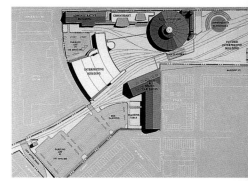

tenance facilities on the property, known as the Mount Clare Shops, were closed and the museum was taken over by an independent nonprofit organization and housed in the 1851 Mount Clare Depot, the 1884 roundhouse and annex, and the 1869 car shop. The roundhouse, a magnificent example of this unusual building type, is suffering from years of deferred maintenance, as is much of the rolling stock.

The ten-year master plan developed by EYP suggests that, with the right financial infusion, the existing resources can be preserved. This would include renovation of 160,000 square feet (14,400 square meters) of buildings. In addition, EYP suggests three new buildings. An 83,500-square-foot (7,515-square-meter) interpretative center would be the forefront building and communicate the museum's key messages about the history of American railroads. The 14,250-square-foot (1,283-square-meter) commissary building would double as a snack bar for museum visitors and a dining room for catered events. Finally, a 34,500-square-foot (3,105-square-meter) storage building, not open to the public, would accommodate as many pieces of rolling stock as possible in conditions that prevent further deterioration. All three buildings would be carefully integrated on the museum's urban site.

For the museum to survive and grow, a major public-relations campaign needs to be undertaken to raise a national constituency. And supporters also need to realize the potential linkage of the museum's site to nearby thriving Inner Harbor.

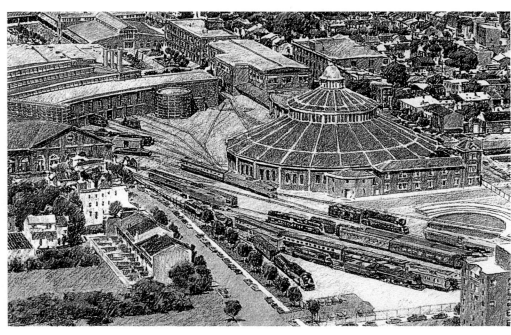

VETERAN'S ADMINISTRATION MEDICAL CENTER

NORTHPORT, NEW YORK

An open-air portico marks the entrance to the new medical center, which sits immediately in front of the existing center.

Established in the 1930s, the Veteran's Administration Medical Center, at Northport, New York, grew into a coherent community of Georgian Revival brick buildings. That was until the 1960s, when a huge, unsympathetic, precast concrete building was inserted into the heart of the 268-acre (107-hectare) complex. Despite that intrusion, the complex was declared a historic district, a fact that was brought to the attention of the selection board when the recent ambulatory-care center was under consideration. That new sensitivity lead to the insertion of a building that respects the historic context of the entire complex and also works to heal the wound the campus received in the 1960s.

The new 90,000-square-foot (8,100-square-meter) ambulatory-care facility was placed along the entire north front of the 1960s building in an attempt to create a new image for this exposure. To reduce the scale, the new building was visually broken down into pieces and appears as two buildings, each with two dominant bays, connected by a central atrium. Facade materials are brick and limestone, to match that of the 1930s facades, and the roof lines are contemporary interpretations of the earlier roofs. A canopied, one-story entranceway that juts forward further breaks up the building's scale.

The new and the old are brought together by a sky-lit atrium that runs down the spine that connects the new ambulatory center with the 1960s building. In the new center, the clinics were designed in a modular arrangement to allow the greatest flexibility. In addition to the new clinic, two existing buildings were renovated and now house 138 psychiatric inpatient beds. All of the facility development had been identified earlier by EYP in a three-stage master facilities plan of the entire campus.

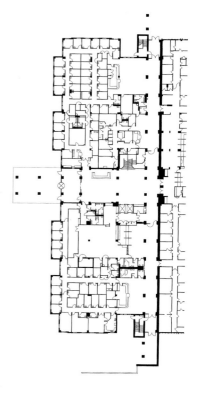

The entrance leads into a large atrium, which flows into a sky-lit pedestrian street that runs perpendicular and connects the new center with the old.

The design of the new medical center sympathetically borrows from the aesthetic language of the entire campus.

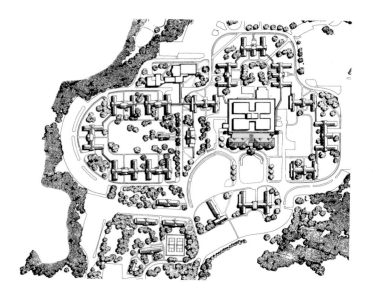

CONGENIAL RESPONSE

INSERTING NEW INTO AN EXISTING ENVIRONMENT

Every architecture firm develops its own signature—certain predilections in style and aesthetics that may change over time but that do so as a continuum. A firm's signature is most evident in the design of new buildings and can run the gamut from highly conservative architecture to architecture that seems to try too hard to be cutting edge. Not surprisingly, the Einhorn Yaffee Prescott signature is greatly influenced by the firm's extensive experience in preservation and in adding new to old. It is a language of response—a thoughtful insertion of a new building into an existing environment. The new is of definite distinction but, at the same time, quietly carries on a congenial conversation with its neighbors.

EYP is conscious of the environment into which the new building will be placed. This consciousness has grown out of necessity. Many of the new buildings are additions to campuses that themselves have evolved slowly over the years. The goal is to renew the spirit of each campus, often adding a new forefront building. Such was the case with the Dana Science Center Addition at Skidmore College and the Marist Student Center at Marist College. The Dana Science Center gently breaks with the architecture of Skidmore's past, while Marist boldly announces a new presence. Yet both rely on a careful study of existing buildings, materials, landscaping, and topography.

Even when cues are taken from the existing buildings, these elements are shifted slightly in an effort to create a new expression. Such was the case with Clark Hall at Hartwick College, a design that sympathetically borrowed from a neighboring historic hall designed by John Russell Pope but that definitively speaks its own language. The materials and massing are similar, yet Clark Hall clearly makes a contemporary statement.

It's rare these days for an architect to design a building that will stand by itself in the middle of a field, especially in the Northeastern and Mid-Atlantic United States, where large tracts of vacant land are a luxury. An important lesson to learn, therefore, is how to skillfully insert a new building onto a site that is surrounded by other distinguished structures and symbols. At SUNY Geneseo, EYP faced a tight site and a requirement on the part of the school to replicate the spirit of the older buildings on campus. The solution skillfully negotiates the sloping site while the design is a future-looking vision. At Gallaudet University, the goal was to visually integrate a large conference center in the context of historic buildings that define the Victorian Gothic quality of this unique campus.

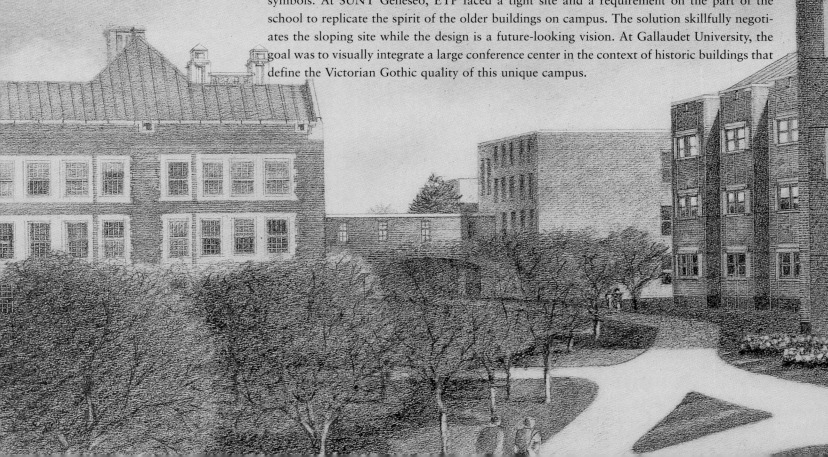

KELLOGG CONFERENCE CENTER, GALLAUDET UNIVERSITY

Inserting a new building in the heart of a historic college campus is chancier when the site is small and the building by necessity is big. Very big. Add a limited budget and some highly unusual requirements, and you've got the formidable list of challenges that faced Einhorn Yaffee Prescott in the design of Kellogg Center at Gallaudet University.

The potential for architectural conflict was clear. This was a 150,000-square-foot (13,500-square-meter), late twentieth-century behemoth on the loose in a neighborhood of nineteenth-century scale. EYP clearly understood that in

this situation you could run but could not hide. The difference in scale might be disguised somewhat, but it wouldn't disappear. Thus, the center takes on the local coloration and camouflages its bulk. You cannot gauge its true size until you are hard upon it, and even then it presents pleasing surprises.

One surprising thing the architects did was to make the five-story building higher than it had to be, topping it with a massive, steep roof echoing that of the Queen Anne-style gymnasium nearby. With its bungalow dormers, the towering roof actually reduces the apparent scale of the four-story rectangle it covers. To minimize its scale, the building picks up the polychrome brickwork of another nineteenth-century building in the area—Wither's powerful College Hall.

Above all, the architects seized every opportunity to squeeze architectural expression out of the site's restrictions and the building's different functions. You have to tuck away from a corner to protect three aging elm trees? Fine, push part of the building back and part forward to make a more interesting shape. Do you need a front door? Yes, indeed, make it an event, a little fortress-like freestanding cylinder. Is there need for a canopy to shield visitors from the rain? Throw in a little deconstructionism (just to show you're up to date) and make it a splendid tilted thing atop steel pillars. Do conference-goers want a place to step outside during breaks? Give that space a roof, and give that roof a big, graceful curve.

Inside the Kellogg Center, one gets the clear impression that an awful lot was done with a little. Remarkably, there are one or two enticing public spaces inside. In front of the auditorium entrance, for example, there's a fine double-height space. But the most interesting facets are those designed especially for the deaf and hard-of-hearing. There are obvious things, such as the availability of special devices for the deaf and hearing-impaired. There also are subtle touches. Colors, for instance, are extremely muted. Lighting in general is a lot brighter—many more incandescent lights than the norm—so that sign language gestures will be seen more clearly. And there are lots of unseen things—extra-thick air ducts to eliminate background noise distraction to people who can hear just a little; extra-powerful climate control units to handle the heat generated by the bright lights. All of this for ninety-two dollars per square foot—more expensive than your backyard shack but a lot cheaper than any other fine institutional building I know of.

The Kellogg Center is a superior example of responsive, and responsible, architecture. It's a building that will give pleasure to many—deaf, partly deaf, and non-deaf.

USER'S VIEW: I. KING JORDAN

KELLOGG CONFERENCE CENTER, GALLAUDET UNIVERSITY

Founded in 1864 in Washington, D.C., Gallaudet University has been dedicated to providing the best possible educational experience to deaf and hard-of-hearing students. The Kellogg Center embodies our long-cherished dream of having a special place designed and dedicated to the continuing educational needs of our community. It was during the heady period of the late 1980s that we approached the W. K. Kellogg Foundation and asked for funding to build a conference center that would enrich Gallaudet's ability to provide professional, continuing

education, and life-skills support to deaf people and those who work with them. It's no coincidence that this occurred on the heels of Gallaudet University's Deaf President Now (DPN) protest that resulted in my becoming the first deaf president of the university and also triggered in deaf people a new sense of self-worth and heightened expectations.

Although we could easily verbalize our requirements and expectations for our new conference center, we relied heavily on Einhorn Yaffee Prescott's commitment to understand and respond to our special needs, and on their innovative design skills to physically shape and bring the project to fruition. And we knew it would be no easy task. We were greatly encouraged during the process when two of EYP's architects spent two weeks living on campus, learning how deaf and hard-of-hearing students learn and interact. This seemed crucial to us. Creating a state-of-the-art facility was a daunting challenge in itself, but to make one sensitive to

the needs of a special population required extraordinary consideration.

This process resulted in a design that seamlessly integrates special amenities for the deaf and hard of hearing. For instance, the building's interior is spatially and visually dynamic and is enriched through the abundance of daylighting, which creates an ever-changing environment. Background colors are muted so that users can easily communicate through sign language—and from different floors in the building through the use of mezzanines and multistory spaces. Even the ductwork was insulated to eliminate noise frequency that is distracting to a person who is hearing impaired. And the building is technologically loaded with systems meant to ease communication, such as strobe lights used as emergency warnings and doorbells and beds that vibrate in case of fire emergency. Because the building is used as a national and international conference center, it contains two floors of hotel rooms to accommodate out-of-town visitors, which is a tremendous added value.

We were pleased that EYP was able to sensitively integrate this large facility into our historic campus without it dominating the existing smaller-scale buildings.

Since its dedication, the Kellogg Center has become more than just a facility aimed at helping the deaf and hard-of-hearing expand their horizons. It is also a place where hearing people can come to learn about deaf people and their culture. This added value attracts a large number of hearing groups who appreciate the building's physical qualities, as well as its unique elements that are less tangible. Thanks to the outstanding design work of EYP, the new facility allows us to reach out to all and offer a place where all people can meet, learn, and interact on equal ground.

KELLOGG CONFERENCE CENTER, GALLAUDET UNIVERSITY

WASHINGTON, D.C.

The size of the large conference center was reduced by its T shape, which works to create a formal courtyard facing the campus's historic quad. The design reinterprets the older buildings' aesthetics.

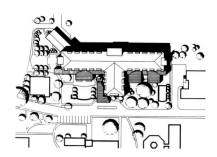

Not only is Gallaudet University proud of its educational mission but also of its architectural heritage. Founded more than a century ago, it is the only university in the world devoted exclusively to educating the deaf and hard-of-hearing. Its original campus quad was master-planned by Frederick Law Olmsted and around it sits historic Victorian structures. When the plan to create the world's first conference center for the deaf and hearing-impaired gained the financial backing of the Kellogg Foundation—and the decision was made to locate it on the edge of the historic quad—Gallaudet turned to Einhorn Yaffee Prescott to skillfully insert the mammoth new building without disturbing the historic fabric of the campus.

From the beginning, one of EYP's main objectives was to visually reduce the size of the Kellogg Center's 150,000-square-foot (13,500-square-meter) allotment. This was accomplished by means of a T-shaped footprint, the stem of the T creating a forecourt facing the historic campus. The massing of Kellogg Center responds more congenially to its immediate neighbor, a high Victorian gymnasium, the second oldest in the country. At the same time, the building's enormity is encountered only at the back facade, which faces toward the edge of campus and is rarely viewed. In a conscious effort to sympathetically recall the aesthetics of the historic campus while not mimicking them, EYP borrowed materials, patterns, forms, and colors found in neighboring Victorian buildings—steep roof shapes and dormer windows with slate-gray shingles, tri-colored horizontal brick banding, accentuated eaves, and a round entry.

Creating a state-of-the-art training and conference center was a challenge for EYP but not one they hadn't faced before (a similar effort was undertaken for General Electric). The new variable in the equation, however, came with satisfying users' unique needs. To better determine these needs, two EYP architects lived on campus for two weeks and discovered that color, motion, and lighting take on weighted importance for the deaf and hard-of-hearing. Design decisions directly

reflect these discoveries. Illumination is brighter than usual throughout the facility so that sign language can be seen without eyestrain. Natural light is introduced through floor-height windows and is able to penetrate deep into the building through interior wall and floor cutouts. Colors are muted to provide a soft background for interpersonal communications. And the architects discovered that motion is music for the deaf. Therefore, the fountain in the lobby provides a visual song for the building's users.

With ninety-three double-occupancy guest rooms and suites located on the fourth and fifth floors, as well as extensive conference facilities, Kellogg Center is a complete learning and training facility. The most public spaces are on the first and second floors—a 274-seat auditorium, a three-hundred-person subdividable ballroom that opens onto a dining room, fourteen meeting/training rooms, an interactive tiered classroom, and a teleconferencing production/meeting room. The entire facility is connected internally and externally through advanced communication systems integrated into the building's design.

Designing in an existing context was a driving force behind the Kellogg Center because of its proximity to historic structures, such as the Victorian gymnasium.

The state-of-the-art center features a 274-seat auditorium, conference rooms, classrooms, and café. All are interconnected via an advanced communication system that emanates from the control room. The interior allows for clear sight lines for interaction among the deaf and hard-of-hearing students (below and opposite).

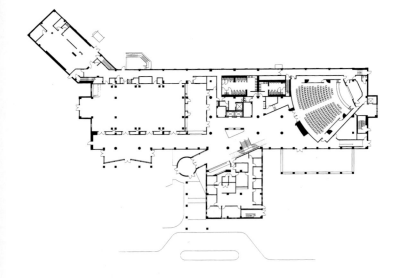

Dr. Joseph J. Bulmer Telecommunications and Computations Center, Hudson Valley Community College

Troy, New York

The communications tower evokes a clear statement about the building's technological mission and draws students and corporations to the school's interactive distance-learning center.

Dramatically marked by a gleaming communications tower, the Bulmer Center, in Troy, New York, signals a bold new direction for this community college in the Hudson River Valley—interactive distance learning. The architecture enhances that mission by taking its cues from the highly technological nature of the center's programs.

The Bulmer Center was conceived as a building that would accommodate all aspects of interactive distance learning. Directly under the communications antennae, the entrance is a glassy box—a multistory space that serves as a lobby to the 250-seat auditorium, as well as to the two wings of classrooms and offices. The auditorium is a one-story curved form that nestles against the classroom wing and is easily identified by visitors to the campus. It is a sophisticated conference center with full video and data connectivity and state-of-the-art display and presentation capabilities. Together with the adjacent function support areas and breakout rooms, this portion of the building responds to the increasing corporate and public demand for large group teleconferencing and satellite down links.

Likewise, the rest of the building is completely wired. The three-story wing has twenty-four classrooms, each built on raised-access flooring, which allows maximum reconfiguring flexibility. In that same wing is the Center for Effective Teaching, consisting of two dedicated classrooms equipped with fifteen computer workstations. The other wing houses the videography/photography area—two fully equipped television studios and an audio studio. The control room allows for distribution around the center and the campus and to remote locations via satellite, microwave, and fiber-optic cable.

Inside, a large, naturally lit atrium serves as a gathering place for students and others attending sessions in the building's auditorium. The media screen, located in the atrium, can display the presentation occurring simultaneously in the auditorium.

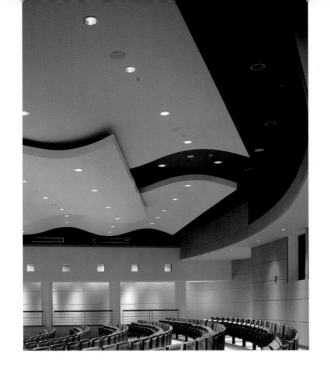

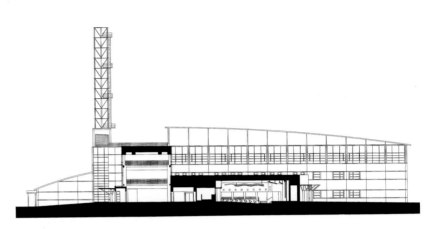

The building is a composition of bold shapes—the vertical tower, transparent entrance, curved auditorium, and classroom wing.

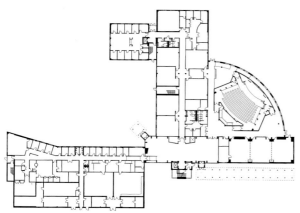

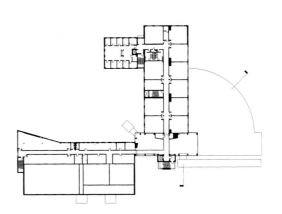

Academic Building and Computer Center, State University of New York, Geneseo

Geneseo, New York

Inserting a contemporary building that respected the collection of existing Collegiate Gothic buildings at SUNY's Geneseo campus was the task facing Einhorn Yaffee Prescott. To complicate matters, the site chosen for the new academic building and computer center was complex—a downhill-slanted parcel tucked tightly among existing buildings but set at a prominent edge of the academic community.

For the center's design, EYP took cues from the original buildings and, in fact, strove to reinforce the strengths of those structures. Borrowed elements include the cupolas, lanterns, and towers, and even the distinctive roof shapes featured on each wing. The goal was to capture the spirit of the place and to visually tie together the new and the old.

The building's Y shape was site driven. To understand its design, think first of an L-shape in which two wings set at a 45-degree angle house the bulk of the interior spaces. The L is connected at each end to existing buildings, of which one link is a dramatic bridge over an access street. Now, add

The building's southwest edge is marked by a prominent tower that echoes roofscapes found on existing campus buildings.

to the L a short leg, in effect making it a Y. Then, foot the Y with a tower offering magnificent long views out over the Genesee Valley. Located at the southwest corner of the campus, the tower serves as a beacon for pedestrian traffic coming from the residential portion of the campus. Students enter into a small courtyard formed off one side of the Y stem and fronted by a colonnade. The entry leads directly into a tall, thin atrium, which slices up through the building, visually unifying the space and allowing natural light to penetrate deep into the building. A larger courtyard sits at the intersection of the L joint and uses the natural slope to become an outdoor amphitheater. To enrich its use, a portion of the building's facade was covered in precast concrete to serve as a giant outdoor projection screen.

A small entrance court is tucked next to the building and leads inside to a thinly proportioned but light-filled atrium. The atrium slices up through the building, providing visual and physical access.

The largest of the two court-yards doubles as an outdoor amphitheater with a concrete projection screen on the building's facade (opposite, top). An enclosed bridge connects the center with the neighboring building.

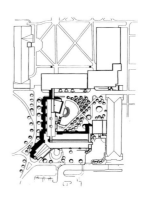

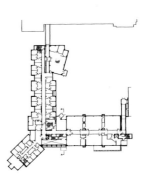

RESIDENCE HALL, LAFAYETTE COLLEGE

EASTON, PENNSYLVANIA

Set on the crest of a hill, the design of the new residence hall embraces the campus's prevailing Georgian style but is decidedly contemporary.

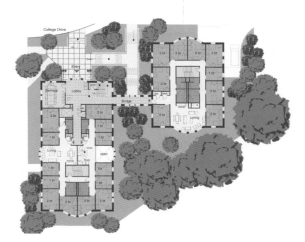

Lafayette College's new residence hall will sit at the crest of a hill and welcome visitors as they approach the school from Easton. For many an architect, the chance to design such a forefront building could result in a building that makes more of a personal statement about that architect's preference than an attempt to enrich the architectural spirit of the campus. For Einhorn Yaffee Prescott, the opportunity is simply another to illustrate the firm's philosophy of congenial response—to delicately and sensitively insert a new building into an existing environment—a building that is a successful work of architecture in itself but also one that doesn't visually or physically interrupt the context of the existing community.

The building's design embraces the Georgian style that prevails in the nearby residence halls yet is decidedly contemporary. Materials include brick, slate pitched roofs, projecting end bays, punched double-hung windows with limestone lintels and sills, and chimneys. Consisting of two wings, the 37,800-square-foot (3,400-square-meter) residence hall will contain several special-interest "houses" or living areas that can accommodate ten to twenty students each. Each house will combine single and double rooms with living and kitchen space and shared bathrooms.

A unique expression is achieved through the building's response to site. Because of the sloping site, one wing is five stories high and contains two-level houses; the other wing is four stories of one-level houses with a common area below. The wings are connected on three levels by a bridge containing lounge space. Other special features include a library/living room just beyond the main entry, two seminar rooms, and a large multipurpose room for academic and social functions. A two-bedroom faculty resident apartment and a one-bedroom head resident apartment are included.

COBLESKILL-RICHMONDVILLE CENTRAL SCHOOL DISTRICT HIGH SCHOOL

COBLESKILL, NEW YORK

The various elements of the Cobleskill High School design combine to give the campus the feeling of a small village. To reflect the character of the surrounding farm community, the gymnasium and theater borrow from the vernacular design of local barn structures.

For the design of a new high school on the outskirts of a well-established farming community, Einhorn Yaffee Prescott looked to rural vernacular building forms. At the same time, through this contextual design, EYP sought to visually express the different functions of the school through unique architectural elements.

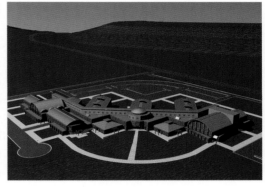

In concept, the high-school is a village, with the educational components informing the various buildings in that village. The design is meant to evoke a regional identity and character. Borrowed for the high school village is the predominant vernacular vaulted barn structure, which at the school becomes two separate prominent elements housing the gymnasium and an eight-hundred-seat theater. At the heart of the 165,000-square-foot (14,850-square-meter) building is a domed, two-story media center, with classroom wings radiating from the media center. Each special teaching area takes on a different form, all of which are visually integrated into the larger whole.

EYP has been commissioned by the Cobleskill-Richmondville Central School District to undertake facility programming and planning, with an emphasis on the exploration of building options to satisfy the district's new and existing facility requirements, as well as a variety of operations and maintenance projects.

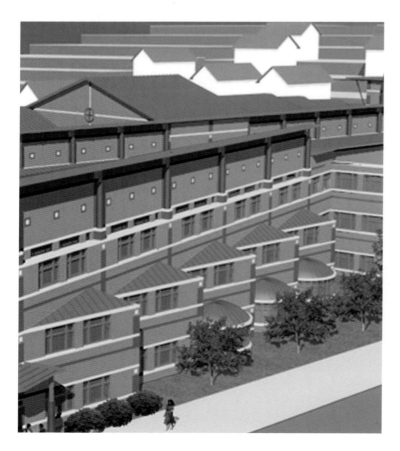

A digital observatory that is contiguous with a clerestory lantern is the focal point of the Paterson, New Jersey, magnet school for science and technology.

PATERSON, NEW JERSEY

The design of the new magnet school for the fine and performing arts revolves around a central element or hinge, from which emanates the educational wing, media center, and gymnasium/theater.

Einhorn Yaffee Prescott's conceptual designs for two new magnet schools are based on similar goals that differ in their architectural expression. The goal was to provide two 140,000-square-foot (12,600-square-meter) schools that congenially responded to the mixed commercial/residential character of the urban sites and also distinctly expressed the unique mission of each school.

The magnet school for science and technology, grades kindergarten through five, is a linear north/south footprint built on the site of a former leather-tanning plant. A prekindergarten day-care facility is a single-story element arching across the north/south axis. Three-stories tall, the building's aesthetics will reflect the urban character of the community, as well as announce its technological focus.

Respectfully, the classrooms will face the residential area, a quieter program with minimal traffic. The gymnasium, theater, media center, and café will face the more commercial side, all of which can be accessed after hours and allow for increased use by the community. The focal point is the observatory, which is contiguous with a clerestory lantern that brings natural light into the heart of the circulation space by day and is a beacon of light by night. The design also delineates different educational levels and expresses their varying square-footage allotments. For the kindergarten rooms, bay windows become storytelling nooks. First- and second-grade rooms are identified by a sawtooth design; the other classrooms have a less pronounced facade.

The second school is a magnet school for the fine and performing arts, grades kindergarten through eight. Its design takes a horseshoe shape, with the playground tucked inside. The courtyard is bounded on the south by a prekindergarten facility, on the west by a classroom block, and on the north by the gymnasium/theater/cafeteria. The focal point of the courtyard is the media center, the rotunda of which visually acts as a hinge in the design. Grades two through seven are housed in suites, each containing a classroom set between separate teaching areas for the fine arts and performing arts. In the design, the classrooms are cantilevered from the main structure and supported by a single column, like a tree house. The site slopes down away from the residential neighborhood, allowing those two facades to be one-story high. On the more commercial side, the school assumes a three-story height.

DANA SCIENCE CENTER ADDITION, SKIDMORE COLLEGE

SARATOGA SPRINGS, NEW YORK

Set at the gateway to the main campus, the center features a curved, glass atrium wall, the shape of which resembles a catcher's mitt. The gesture is meant as a way of welcoming visitors to the campus.

The design of the Dana Science Center Addition brought a dual, sometimes contradictory, challenge to Einhorn Yaffee Prescott. Not only was it to be a forefront building showcasing the sciences at Skidmore College, but it also needed to be in sympathetic alignment with the rest of the campus, a grouping of relatively new buildings that had been designed by one architect.

Once located in downtown Saratoga Springs, Skidmore College developed a new campus on the outskirts of town in the 1960s. One architectural style dominated—brick-fronted buildings with thin slot windows. True to its inclination toward congenial response, EYP chose to borrow from the aesthetic language of these original buildings. Influential were the slotted window patterns, roof overhangs, and detailing, as well as the use of brick. Because the Dana Science Center was meant to bring a much-needed presence to the sciences on campus, the building needed its own identity, and a strong one at that.

Dana's uniqueness is expressed in a curved, glass atrium wall, the shape of which evokes the image of a catcher's mitt. The transparency of that wall, especially at night, beckons to students and visitors and gives the impression that the brick is peeling back. In fact, Dana Science Center has become a forefront building, located at a gateway to the main campus.

Inside, the curved wall fronts a prominent atrium space where students and faculty come together. As a symbolic gesture, the names of prominent scientists run in bands along the wall and reference the subject matter taught in the science center—geology, physics, chemistry, and biology. The decorative elements of the highly articulated atrium also reflect a scientific theme—African slate on the floor (as a metaphor for earth) and whiter surfaces up above (as a metaphor for clouds). So successful is this grand space, it is used for a variety of student functions and has added a good deal of value to the Skidmore campus.

The atrium becomes a show-place for the sciences, as well as a gathering place for students and faculty of all academic concentrations. The labs are highly flexible in design to allow for easy rearrangement.

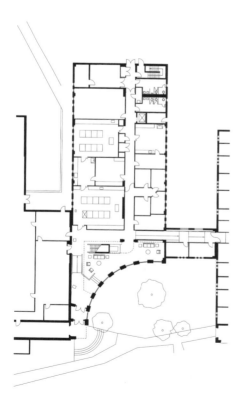

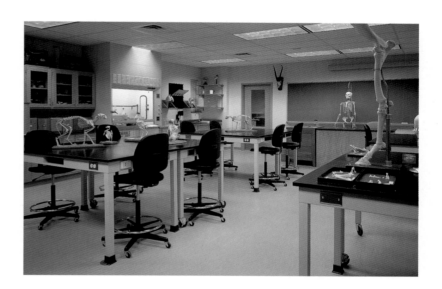

SKIDMORE HALL, SKIDMORE COLLEGE

SARATOGA SPRINGS, NEW YORK

On a campus predominately comprising buildings constructed of one material—brick—Skidmore Hall presents a unique image with its repetitive dominant bays, brick, and assemblage of thin, blue-painted, steel add-ons. Yet it maintains a congenial relationship with neighboring buildings.

The design of a new residence hall at Skidmore College again illustrates Einhorn Yaffee Prescott's theme of congenial response. Its aesthetics build on—and advance—the architecture of the entire Skidmore campus. A critical goal of the project was to create a residence hall that would provide an attractive environment for learning beyond the classroom.

When EYP was hired to design Skidmore Hall, all the residence halls on campus had been designed by another firm and were consistent in appearance. (Skidmore's campus was relatively new, having moved from a downtown site.) What EYP sought was a "gentle departure" from the old design language, a subtle shift from the past. So for congeniality, the new residence hall borrows red brick, repetitive bay windows, and flat roofs from the nearby residence halls. But the expression is uniquely different. The bays become projecting steel forms painted black. The use of steel is repeated—although this time painted blue—at the building entrances and to distinguish the interior common spaces. The building's configuration

is also unique—a thin serpentine shape that turns through the site, allowing natural light into and views out onto the wooded site and causing minimal destruction to the mature landscape. A dramatic departure was made in the interior design—the inclusion of a large conference room in an attempt to bring the faculty to the students. Single and double bedrooms were carefully placed amid common rooms of a variety of shapes and functions—again, to encourage social interaction among students but also with faculty members.

The building's serpentine shape allows an abundance of natural light into all the interior spaces—bedrooms, lounges, and dining areas—and offers a proliferation of views out to the wooded grounds.

CLARK HALL, HARTWICK COLLEGE

Although more contemporary in design, Clark Hall sits in sympathetic discourse with neighboring Bresee Hall, Hartwick College's historic centerpiece designed by John Russell Pope.

In the early 1900s, noted American architect John Russell Pope applied his genius to creating a master plan for Hartwick College, a small, liberal-arts school dramatically situated on a steep hill that overlooks the town of Oneonta. Pope designed the centerpiece Bresee Hall, a Neo-Georgian red brick and limestone academic building, and designated the plot next to it for a future academic building. That design task fell to Einhorn Yaffee Prescott, who in turn, approached the problem by sensitively reinterpreting Pope's vision into a contemporary design. The goal was to respect and respond to Pope's master plan and design vocabulary yet signal that the new learning center—Clark Hall—represented a different era in education.

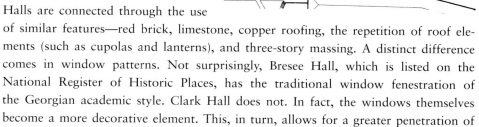

Visually, Clark and Bresee Halls are connected through the use of similar features—red brick, limestone, copper roofing, the repetition of roof elements (such as cupolas and lanterns), and three-story massing. A distinct difference comes in window patterns. Not surprisingly, Bresee Hall, which is listed on the National Register of Historic Places, has the traditional window fenestration of the Georgian academic style. Clark Hall does not. In fact, the windows themselves become a more decorative element. This, in turn, allows for a greater penetration of natural light into the interiors.

The flooding of light is most pronounced in the glassy, projecting entry pavilions that flank the building on its north and south ends and act as a counterpoint to the window design. Stacked in the north pavilion from bottom to top are a faculty center, a writing center, and a seminar room. The south pavilion contains a full-height atrium and a monumental stairway. It is a warm, welcoming entry into the learning center, its walls painted white with wood window frames left in their natural color. This color scheme highlights the tactile, domestic quality of the wood. And when the sun moves across the sky, the tonality of the wood changes. Accessed from the atrium on the third floor, an enclosed bridge links Clark Hall with historic Bresee Hall and frames picturesque views out over the Susquehanna Valley.

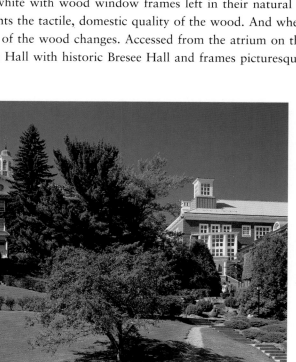

Set on the crest of a steep hill overlooking the city of Oneonta, Clark Hall's multitude of windows and glassy entry pavilions admit an abundance of natural light inside and views out. A bridge accessed on the north side of the atrium's third floor links Clark and Bresee Halls.

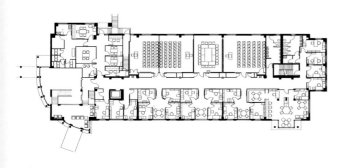

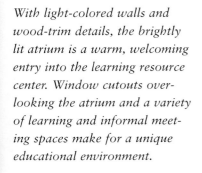

With light-colored walls and wood-trim details, the brightly lit atrium is a warm, welcoming entry into the learning resource center. Window cutouts overlooking the atrium and a variety of learning and informal meeting spaces make for a unique educational environment.

MARIST COLLEGE STUDENT CENTER
AND RESIDENCE HALL

The Marist Student Center overlooks a newly formed campus green. Stepping down the site toward the river is the new residence hall. The rotunda, which glows at night, has become a focal point of the campus. Large, glassy surfaces admit an abundance of natural light into the atrium, dining, and activity areas.

Formerly a seminary overlooking the Hudson River, in Poughkeepsie, New York, Marist College inherited a collection of high-quality, small-scale brick and stone buildings when it established itself as a private, liberal-arts school. What it lacked was a master plan with a central focal point. Einhorn Yaffee Prescott brought to Marist a traditional campus organization couched in contemporary garb. Now, reflective of the classic Jeffersonian campus, a colonnaded rotunda stands at the edge of the campus green. Instead of the Jeffersonian marble-clad rotunda, however, this is a highly transparent one, constructed of anodized aluminum columns set around a glassy core. The rotunda is topped with a glass dome—green glass to act as a solar canopy. Casting a silvery gleam during the day and glowing at night, the rotunda has become the gateway to the campus, a strong architectural element that establishes a point of arrival.

Inside, the rotunda explodes into a huge, brightly lit central space. Wrapping around its perimeter, a stair and bridge system allows visual access inside and out. The rotunda also serves as a circulation spine, with the student center off one side and the residence hall off the other. Like the rotunda, the student center features a dramatic, multistory, natural lit space, which has become a special activity room for the entire campus. The new residence hall is sited perpendicular to the Hudson River to maximize views out over the water and down the hill to the river. The residence hall is actually a series of "little houses," three-story elements that push in and out. A protective colonnade along the lowest level follows the site's topography and invites pedestrian traffic down the hill.

The placement of the entire complex was critical to the master plan of the campus. Eventually, across the green, a new library will be built. But even without the library, the site is considerably more welcoming than it was in its former incarnation as a parking lot. The new green in front of Marist Student Center is designed for campus-wide, outdoor activities and has a podium that overlooks the river.

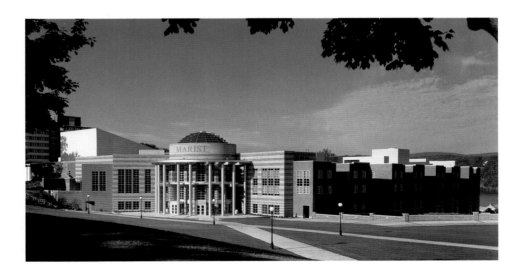

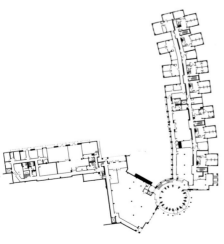

The student center(above)and the rotunda, with its broad and central stairs and views to the campus, have become symbols for the campus community and popular gathering places. At dusk, Marist Center becomes a silvery beacon on campus.

Firm Collaborators

Many thanks to the following people whose hard work and commitment to design excellence have contributed to the success of Einhorn Yaffee Prescott.

Patrick J. Abbott
John Acheampong
Larry G. Adams
Michael D. Adams
Harold Adler
Deborah Akel
James A. Albach
Jeffrey M. Albert
Christine M. Alestock
Marcia G. Allen
Sabreen M. Allyn
Azhar Ameen
Indu Anand
Jagdish C. Anand
Eric L. Anderson
Dante B. Anoia
Victoria C. Armsby
Leonid Arnopolin
Thomas R. Ashley
Izrail Asinovsky
Warren W. Askland
Thomas S. Assimon
Mouloud Atoui
Joyce A. Audi
Antoinette Ayres
Ronald L. Bagoly
James J. Baker
Jonathan K. Balas
Sandra M. Baptie
Richard J. Barcori
Larry E. Barker, Jr.
Kristine Barr
Katie Barrett
John R. Baxter
Daniel Beaton
Susan V. Beggerow
Meghan L. Belcher
Paul J. Benanti
Stephen Bender
Paul J. Benoit
Carlos Bent
Lucille F. Benz
Angela D. Berry
Richard J. Bertani
Diane I. Bessette
Donald B. Betton
Julie M. Bierlein
Deborah T. Birch
Tom D. Birdsey
Alan Black
Lawrence R. Blanche
Mikhail Bleykhman
John S. Bogdanski
Catherine N. Boggs
Stephane Boigris
Gopinath K. Boray
Jason A. Borrelli
Donald L. Bosserman
John W. Bossung, Jr.
Linda L. Boyer
Angela K. Bradshaw
Lauren D. Bradshaw
Jose Luis Brenes

Michelle C. Brent
Brian K. Brobst
George Lewis Brode, III
Nancy A. Brown
Nathan K. Brown
Thelma L. Brown
Lisa R. Brukner
John Bruno
Richard K. Buckley
Beth D. Buffington
Thomas J. Bunszell
Maria-Beatriz Buot
Brenda Burke
Donald Burns
Joseph S. Bushey, Jr.
Joann (Gale) Buttacavoli
Joseph L. Calvarese
John D. Capra
Jean A. Capuano
Nicholas Capuano
Marvis Sherrie Carey
Pamela J. Carroll
T. Scott Carter
Clare C. Chapman
Glaiston Chen
Eu Hock Chuah
Sun Y. Chung
John B. Churchill
Kathy Cino
Aaron G. Clark
David L. Clemenzi
Hennison Clovis
Anthony Cobuzzi
Rosemary L. Cobuzzi
David Brooks Coe
Timothy Cohan
Randolph Collins
Christine Conboy
Michele C. Conway
Kathryn A. Coogan
Dale C. Coon
Patti-Jane Cooper
Anthony Coschigano
Roger Cote
Thomas P. Coughlin
Stephen B. Coulston
David J. Courtemanche
Robert Cousins
Lee F. Cox
William Craft
Diane Cramer
Samuel A. Cravotta
Maria Cristina Crosetto
Karen A. Cross
Benjamin W. Crowley
James J. Cruger
Richard F. Cunningham
Patrick Curley
Chad J. Czelusniak
James Eric Dahl
John Damalas
John D'Avanzo
Glenn Oliver Davis, Jr.

Deborah M. De Luca
Nancy Chang Decker
Paul Sean Delave
David Dembling
Snehal R. Desai
Jeanne L. Devoe
Steve Dimovski
Andrew Dinobile
Kwafo Djan
Marian K. Dombroski
Andrew Domian
Kelly L. Donahue
Brian J. Donnelly
William A. Donnelly
Chantal Dorrance
William J. Dougherty
Dennis Drozd
Eileen M. Duggan
James P. Dunlavey
Joseph B. Durham, II
Anele Dzekciorius
Marion G. Eaker
Franklin S. Ebbert
Lisa Marie Eberhart
John S. Edwards
Robert C. Eichelman
Lee Einhorn
Marc Einhorn
Sherry Einhorn
Steven L. Einhorn
Khalil R. Eldana
Salvatore S. Elder
Michael Elia
Lloyd Eliseo
Cheryl Elmer
Kathleen M. Eltman
Marie T. Ennis
Charles E. Enos
Marketa Esaili
Kevin Eskandary
Jeffrey M. Esposito
Veronica Evangelista
Larry P. Evans
Harry M. Falconer, Jr.
George T. Farnum
Roy H. Feinzig
John J. Felber
Lance E. Ferson
Nicola D. Ferzacca
Lisa B. Fiedorek
Thomas J. Fisher
Joane Fitzpatrick
Meg A. Fitzsimmons
Brian M. Fletcher
James E. Flynn
Lamonte M. Fowler
Michael E. Fowler
Jane Y. Franklin
Glenn G. Frazier
Michael C. Fries
Robin Fritzsche
David M. Funaro
Derek W. Gallardo

Wilfredo M. Gan
Charlotte A. Gannon
David Garceau
Paul A. Garrison
Hamid R. Garzan
John L. Gaudio
Dena Gauthier
Douglas E. Gehley
James F. Gerou, Jr.
Richard T. Gerrity
Ralph Arthur Giammatteo
Pamela M. Gibbons
Kevern Gladstone
J. Lee Glenn
Edwin J. Glover
Anna Goldberg
Craig D. Goldberg
Patrick Golden
Zakeha Gooden
Kimberly A. Gottfredson
Robert L. Grant
Pierre Gravel
Carter B. Green
Peter Gross
Richard Gruft
Michael J. Guerard
David H. Guilder
Robert Guillaume
Ferda L. Guzey
John William Hall
Joyce M. Hallinan
Margaret A. Hamil
Antoinette Hamilton
Christopher Hamilton
Margaret S. Hamilton
Edward C. Hammond
Amy E. Hardt
David P. Harmic
John R. Hathaway
Anthony A. Hauck
Randall Hay
Paula J. Hayward
Gregory Haze
Virginia A. Heald
James M. Healey
Lisa J. Hellmuth
Mark T. Hemingway
Luc Herbots
Gaius B. Hershey
Ryane Hickok
Debbie L. High
Alison H. Hill
Lee Hilton
Dennis W. Holder
Deborah R. Holveg
Kofi Senyo Honu
Alfred K. Hooten
William D. Houdek
Kevin P. Houley
Karen S. Houseknecht
Stephen D. Huang
A. Patricia Hughes
Celina Hung

Robert D. Hunsberger
Charles R. Hunter
James M. Hunter
Tracy A. Hunter
Bernard J. Huss
Cin M. Huynh
Douglas B. Hyde
James E. Igoe, Jr.
Geza P. Illes
Ellen J. Imhof
Vicki M. Indilicato
Milton G. Iriarte
Nathan C. Isley
Stephanie Itkin
Trisha A. Izzo
Robert W. Jansen
Frank Jelley
Arthur Jettelson
Dante Jimenez
Craig G. Johansen
Dennis Johnson
Jeannette M. Johnson
Sarajane Johnson
Joy L. Jordan
Sandra Kanner
Arthur R. Kaplan
Sandra D. Karge
Glori F. Keller
Elissa L. Kellett
Carol A. Kelley
John R. Kells
David A. Kemnitzer
Mark E. Kemp
Raisa Kendall
Eric M. Kern
Susan L. Kerns
Patricia F. Kerwood
Mohammad I. Khan
Shahid R. Khawaja
Thomas K. C. Khoo
Soon Ock Kim
Robert W. King
Charles J. Kirby
Edward C. Kirby
Richard B. Kitch, Jr.
Barbara J. Kleimola
James J. Kleimola
Judy Klein
Charles Koester
Edmund F. Kohlberg
Wendy A. Krivitzky
Richard Kuhn
Christopher Kurkjian
Daniel M. LaBreck
Beth Ellen Lacey
Christopher J. Lacroix
Alana I. Ladd
Gary Lam
Mark A. Landon
Richard D. LaRose
Michelle R. Lasken
Hugh Latimer
Kristine R. Latimer

MELVIN L. LATIMER
LARRY LAU
WILLIAM P. LAVINE
KATHERINE R. LEMOS
ANTHONY LEVA
RICHARD S. LEVINE
DELROY A. LEWIS
SCOTT LEWIS
LING LI
WEI LI
DEBRA S. LIETZ
PAUL LIGNITI
CRISTIAN A. LILLO
LAWRENCE A. LINDER
PAUL I. LINDSEY
DONNA R. LITTLECOOK
DANIEL LLAVE
MICHAEL LO
LEO LOCKER
AHMADWALI LODIN
ARTHUR C. LOHSEN
SUSAN M. LOHSEN
TERESA K. LONG
ALFRED LONGO
ROBERT LOPEZ
JOAN M. LORD
THOMAS B. LUCAS
HERMAN LUTZ
MARY ANNE LYDON
PATRICK T. LYDON
CRAIG N. LYMAN
SEAN M. LYONS
BIENVENIDO MACARAEG
GEOFFREY L. MACDONALD
CARL E. MACINTOSH, JR.
JUDITH M. MACK
HARRY W. MACPHERSON
DEAN E. MAGLIERI
ANTHONY C. MAISANO
ADAM MAJOR
CLAUDINE MALCOLM
LYNDA MANCINI-DIVALENTIN
JOSEPH T. MANGAN, JR.
GEORGE K. MARSHALL
THERESA M. MARSHALL
VIKTOR MARTAUS
JOSEPH N. MARTINOLICH
STEPHEN J. MASKELL
LOUIS MASTRANGELO
ERWIN B. MATE
FLORESCENA MATIBAG
ROBERT MAYERS
DANIEL D. MCARDLE
EUGENE J. MCARDLE
DENNIS MCCAFFREY
SUSAN B. MCCLYMONDS
PATRICIA A. MCCREADY
JOHN M. MCDONALD
ALIX A. MCDONOUGH
GARTH V. MCDONOUGH
MICHELE A. MCGLEW
CHRISTOPHER M. MCGRATH
SYDNEY L. MCGRATH

JAMES I. MCKINNEY
JAMES F. MCLAUGHLIN, III
ROBERTA A. MCLAUGHLIN
DOUGLAS K. MCLELLAN
JUDITH M. MCNEALUS
KIM D. MCTARNAGHAN
CHRISTOPHER J. MEIGEL
NESTOR A. MIJARES
MICHAEL J. MILLS
ANTHONY H. MIMIAGA
JOHN A. MISSELL
MICHAEL C. MITCHELL
SOHEILA MOBASHERAN
HOSEIN M. MORAVEJI
NECHESA A. MORGAN
KEVIN F. MORIARTY
THOMAS J. MORRISSEY
HOMAYOON MORTAZAVI
WANDA MUNOZ-PEREZ
DAVID MURATORE
PATRICIA M. MURPHY
ROBERT A. MUSCATELLO
JOHN WAYNE MYERS
RICHARD S. NAAB
RANJAN NAMBIAR
KHOSROW NAMDAR
GENNADIY NARODITSKY
JESSICA ELAINE NEDD
ANTHONY NELSON
CHRISTOPHER J. NEWTON
FRANCINE V. NUNEZ
JEFFREY L. NUTTER
DAVID OBOLER
SUNG-JIN OH
PIERO OLIVERI
SUSAN BOYD OLLIS
JUDAH ORGANIC
JILL ORLOV
NANCY M. ORMSBY-FLYNN
JEAN M. O'TOOLE
SARAH O'TOOLE
JOHN PANETTA
SCOTT J. PASKE
BENJAMIN J. PASLEY, JR.
KATHLEEN B. PATTERSON
ELENE GILLESPIE PAUL
VALERIE R. PAUL
WILLIAM E. PENNOCK
JERALD PEPPER
AMY J. PHILLIPS
PAUL PIAZZA
DANIEL B. PIERCE
DEBRA T. PIERRE-LOUIS
HEATH P. PITCHERALLE
JOHN S. POCOROBBA
ALICIA R. POLLAK
DEBORAH W. POODRY
KITTIPUN POONJUMNERN
JOSEPH W. PORCELLI
KENNETH D. POSTELL
LOEL C. POTENTE
MILTON PRATT
MARK B. PRENDERGAST

ANDREW W. PRESCOTT
JANIPP M. PRIETO
DORINA RADU
SUSAN R. RADZYMINSKI
AMIR RAOUFI
MARK W. RAYMOND
DANIEL K. REDMOND
GEORGE REHL
CHARLES J. REID
JOSEPH B. REID
JAMIE REINHARDT
MICHAEL R. REITANO
BARBARA A. REUTER
TEOFILO V. REYES
MARLENE M. REYNOLDS
GITI RIAZI
RICHARD W. RICE
HARRIET RIFKIN
CHARLES J. RINALDO
RONALD RITORTO
WALTER RITTER
DAVID RIVERA
JONATHAN E. RIVERA
MICHAEL A. RIZZO
MARKUS V. ROBINSON
IRENE F. ROCKENSTIRE
MAURICIO RODRIGUEZ
STEFANIE H. ROMANOWSKI
JONATHAN B. ROMIG
SAMUEL L. ROSE
WILLIAM A. ROSE, JR.
KENDRA JO ROSS
STEFAN ROSSI
NICHOLAS ROUCHKA
DINA ROZENBLAT
JULIANNE L. RUSSELL
CHARLES J. SACCO
RAMON R. SANTOS
ELSA M. SANTOYO
JEFFREY L. SCHANTZ
DANIEL SCHERMERHORN
JOHN SCHIFF
CHRISTOPHER T. SCHUMAN
PAUL SCOVILLE
JANE SEELEY
MARVIN H. SEGNER
ROSEMARY J. SEIWALD
ORAL A. SELKRIDGE
PAUL SHAPIRO
RONALD SHAPIRO
STEVEN SHAPIRO
CLARK J. SHAUGHNESSY
MARC A. SHAW
ROBERT SHELTON, JR.
DAVID W. SHORT
LYLE R. SHUTE
EWA G. SIADECKI
TIMOTHY SIEVERS
RICHARD C. SIMONS
JENNIFER L. SLAVIK
JAMES A. SLEICHER
ALEXIS SMISLOVA, JR.
DAVID L. SMITH

KENYA K. SMITH
OTIS R. SMITH
JOHN C. SOBIECKI
DAVID SOFER
ANDREW MORGAN SOHN
VEDA N. SOLOMON
VICTOR A. SOUSA
EVELYN SPECIALE TIMBERLAKE
ROBERT J. SPIAK
DAVID E. SPRIGGS
SUKUMAR SRINIVASAN
JASON E. STANCO
EDWARD STAND
MARGARET B. STANLEY
SCOTT B. STECKLER
RALPH STEINGLASS
CAHAL STEPHENS
MICHAEL L. STILE
PAUL A. STOCKERT
JULIUS STONE
JOAN FRANCES STOUFFER
DOMINICK STUART
ROBIN L. STYLES-LOPEZ
STEVEN A. SUNDIUS
GLORIA J. SYDNOR
JORGE SZENDIUCH
GRAZYNA SZYMBORSKI
PURISIMA K. TAN
CHRISTOPHER J. TAVENER
HEATHER H. TAYLOR
MARK E. THALER
JOSEPH J. THOMSON
JOHN B. TINGLEY
JEFFERY E. TISHMAN
SALVATORE N. TOMA
PAMELA L. TORRES
DAT MANH TRAN
MICHAEL J. TRICARICO
JOHN TSAI
JOHN R. TUBMAN
JOANNE TUOSTO
J. LOUIS TURPIN
VINCENT J. TUTTLE
ANN A. TYSON
CENEN C. URCIA
SHARON VAIL
IDA K. VANDERHOOF
PARGEV N. VARDANIAN
CARLOS F. VARELA
ROBERT VECCHIONE
LEONA S. VERSTANDIG
CHRISTINE C. VESCIO
DRAGANA VLATKOVIC
CHARLES R. VOLANS
JOSEPH ALFRED VOLPE
JENNIFER D. WALLER
GLENDON WALSON
MELISSA LEE WALTMAN
JIRAPORN WANAPUN
GLORIA J. WARE
DUSTIN E. WARMUS
CARLTON R. WARNER
LAWRENCE W. WARNER

MARK WARNER
AKIRA WATANABE
DAVID J. WATROBSKI
RENEE R. WAYLAND
JEAN P. WEBSTER
PAMELA SUE WEIGLE
PHILIP WEINBERGER
MARK WELTE
CHRISTINE R. WERNER
RONALD WHATLEY
JEFFREY C. WHELAN
CINDY L. WHITE
LIZABETH A. WHITE
MARION WHITE
HERBERT WIELAND
GEORGE W. WILL, SR.
MARCUS EDWARD WILLIAMS
ROBERT WILLIAMSON
COURTNEY E. WILLIS
SCOTT A. WILSON
TRENT L. WILSON
JOHN WIMMERS
JOSEPH WINTER
LAWRENCE WISBESKI
HENRY W. WOLLER
ANDREW WONG
HING Y. WONG
MARK D. WOODRUFF
JOSEPH M. WOODS
ROBERT J. WOODS
MERVYN J. WOODVILLE
CHIA-HENG WU
ERIC C. YAFFEE
JARED P. YAFFEE
KARYN YAFFEE
MARA B. YAFFEE
STEPHEN C. YAKEY
M. DONALD YAMIN
JOHN H. YARBOROUGH
ANTONIO H. Y. YAU
JEFFREY D. YOUNG
BERNARD P. YOZWIAK
LEONID ZALESHCHANSKIY
TERESA ZANG
JOHN ZANZANO
JAMES ZEBROWSKI
GONG ZHANG
DAVID L. ZOLL
DANIEL J. ZUCZEK

Cover photo
Jeff Goldberg / ESTO

Respectful Response
Drawing of New York State Education
Building from New York State
Archives, pages 12–13

New York State Education Building
Michael Gallitelli, pages 16, 24 (top)
Jeff Goldberg / ESTO, pages 15, 17
(bottom), 18–20, 21 (top), 22–23, 24
(bottom)
Peter Vanderwarker, pages 17 (top) and
25 (top and bottom)

Fleet Bank Corporate Headquarters
Bill Murphy, pages 10 (bottom), 26–27,
29 (bottom), 30 (bottom), 31–34, 35
(top and bottom right)

Old Executive Office Building
Charles Rumph, page 36
Judy Davis / Hoachlander Photography,
page 37
Harlan Hambright, page 39
White House Press Office Archive, page
38 (top left)
Walter Smalling, Jr., pages 11 (top), 40–43
Einhorn Yaffee Prescott, page 38
(bottom left)

Commerce Law Library
Walter Smalling, Jr., pages 44, 45 (top)
Courtesy General Services
Administration, National Capital
Region, page 45 (bottom)

Federal Hall National Memorial
Peter Aaron / ESTO, page 46
Durston Saylor, page 47

Memorial Amphitheater, Arlington
National Cemetary
Walter Smalling, Jr., pages 48, 49 (top),
50–51
Einhorn Yaffee Prescott, page 49 (bottom)

Lincoln and Jefferson Memorials
Christopher Barnes, pages 52, 56 (top
and bottom left), 57
Will & Deni McIntyre / Tony Stone
Images, page 53 (top)
Henley & Savage / Tony Stone Images,
pages 9, 53 (bottom)
Greg Pease / Tony Stone Images, page 55
Einhorn Yaffee Prescott, pages 54, 56
(bottom)

Argus Building
Lance Gardner Biesele, pages 58, 60
(top), 61
Norman McGrath, pages 59, 60
(bottom), 62, 63

General Electric Company World
Customer Reception Center
Peter Vanderwarker, pages 64, 65
(bottom)
Jeff Goldberg / ESTO page 65 (top)
Durston Saylor, pages 66–67

Sage and Williams Halls, Williams College
Nicholas Whitman, pages 68–71
Peter Vanderwarker, pages 72–73

Kirby Hall, Lafayette College
Kevin Worthen / Lafayette College,
page 74
Jim McKinney / Einhorn Yaffee Prescott,
page 75 (top and center)
Courtesy Lafayette College, page 75
(bottom)

NORA RICHTER GREER is a freelance writer living in Washington, D.C. As a communications consultant specializing in architecture and urban affairs, Ms. Greer's work runs the gamut from public relations and marketing to writing and editing newsletters, magazine articles, and books. Previously, she was senior editor at *Architecture Magazine* and editor of the National Trust for Historic Preservation's *Forum* magazine and newsletter. She is the author of two books on housing the homeless, *The Search for Shelter* and *The Creation of Shelter*, published by the American Institute of Architects. A graduate of Connecticut College, Ms. Greer received a master's degree of science in journalism from Northwestern University and is currently completing a master's degree of arts in creative writing at Johns Hopkins University.

THOMAS FISHER is the dean of the College of Architecture and Landscape Architecture at the University of Minnesota. Formerly, he was editorial director of *Progressive Architecture* magazine. With degrees in architecture and intellectual history, Fisher acted as historic architect for the states of Connecticut and Ohio.

WILLIAM KENNEDY is the recipient of numerous literary prizes and awards, including the Pulitzer Prize in 1984 for his novel *Ironweed*. Born in Albany, New York, he began his career as a reporter and over the years performed a wide range of journalistic assignments involving the world of sports, politics, and literature. He began pursuing a full-time career writing fiction in 1961 and since that time has published seven novels: *Ironweed, The Ink Truck, Legs, Billy Phelan's Greatest Game, Quinn's Book, Very Old Bones*, and *The Flaming Corsage*. An accomplished screenwriter, teacher, and children's book author, he founded and directed the New York State Writers Institute at the University of Albany, SUNY, after receiving a prestigious MacArthur Foundation fellowship in 1981.

GORDON AMBACH has served as the executive director of the Council of Chief State School Officers (CCSSO) since July 1987. His leadership at CCSSO followed twenty years of service in the state of New York, as the New York State Commissioner of Education and president of the University of the State of New York and as Executive Deputy Commissioner of Education. The New York State Education Department is the nation's largest and most comprehensive state education agency with responsibility for all public and private elementary, secondary, and high school education; libraries, museums, archives, and historical organizations; vocational rehabilitation; and all professional licensure in the state.

CHARLES LINN is senior managing editor at *Architectural Record*. Before he joined the magazine in 1990, he was editor of *Architectural Lighting* magazine, which he founded in 1986. A licensed architect, Linn received a bachelor's degree of arts in architecture from Kansas State University in 1978.

GEORGE WHITNEY joined the staff of Middlebury College in 1973 and has served as the director of operations since 1983. In addition to providing leadership for the Directors of Facilities Management, Dining Service, New Construction and Major Renovation, Managers of the College Store, Mailing Services, Publications and Reprographics, he has been intimately involved in the adaptive reuse and renovation of 378,000 square feet and shared responsibility for 295,500 square feet of new construction.

BENJAMIN FORGEY is the architecture critic of the *Washington Post*. His essay is adapted from an article that appeared on April 15, 1995, in the *Washington Post*.

I. KING JORDAN became the eighth president of Gallaudet University in 1988 after fifteen years as a faculty member in the Department of Psychology and two years as dean of the College of Arts and Sciences. As the university's first deaf president, he has served as an international spokesperson for deaf and hard-of-hearing people as well as an advocate for persons with disabilities. Dr. Jordan earned a bachelor's degree of arts in psychology from Gallaudet University in 1970, and a master's degree of arts in 1971 and a doctorate in 1973, both in psychology, at the University of Tennessee.